HIGH STYLE

HIGH STYLE

*Masterworks from the Brooklyn Museum Costume Collection
at The Metropolitan Museum of Art*

JAN GLIER REEDER

*The Metropolitan Museum of Art, New York
Yale University Press, New Haven and London*

This volume is published in conjunction with the exhibitions "American Woman: Fashioning a National Identity," on view at The Metropolitan Museum of Art, New York, May 5–August 15, 2010, and "American High Style: Fashioning a National Collection," on view at the Brooklyn Museum, May 7–August 1, 2010.

The exhibition "American Woman: Fashioning a National Identity" at The Metropolitan Museum of Art is made possible by Gap. Additional support is provided by Condé Nast.

Published by The Metropolitan Museum of Art, New York
Gwen Roginsky, General Manager of Publications
Margaret Rennolds Chace, Managing Editor
Joan Holt, Editor
Bruce Campbell, Designer
Douglas Malicki, Production Manager
Robert Weisberg and Carol Liebowitz, Desktop Publishing
Lea Ingold and Lolly Koon, Photographers
Models dressed by Glenn Petersen

Separations by Professional Graphics, Inc., Rockford, Ill.
Printed and bound by Mondadori Printing S.p.A., Verona, Italy

Front cover/jacket: Charles James, *"Tree" Ball Gown*, 1955
Frontispiece: Madeleine Vionnet, *Evening Ensemble*, ca. 1935
Back cover/jacket: Arnold Scaasi, *Evening Ensemble*, 1961

Cataloging-in-Publication Data is available from the Library of Congress.
ISBN 978-1-58839-362-3 (hc: The Metropolitan Museum of Art)
ISBN 978-1-58839-363-0 (pbk: The Metropolitan Museum of Art)
ISBN 978-0-300-15522-8 (hc: Yale University Press)

Contents

Directors' Forewords

High Style: Masterworks from the Brooklyn Museum Costume Collection at The Metropolitan Museum of Art celebrates the landmark partnership of two great New York institutions and marks the culmination of the Brooklyn Museum's comprehensive four-year assessment of their renowned costume collection. With the support of the Andrew W. Mellon Foundation and a team headed by Jan Glier Reeder, the author of this volume and now Consulting Curator at The Costume Institute, the Brooklyn Museum's inventory and survey entailed the evaluation, recataloging, and photographing of more than 24,000 accessioned objects. The remarkable images and much of the research presented in this book are the result of this ambitious project.

High Style, with its examples suggesting the extraordinary diversity of the Brooklyn Museum's costume holdings, is only a small sampling of the rich cache of historic material that comprises the core of the collection. Reeder had the enviable, if challenging, task of selecting not only the most distinguished masterworks from the collection but also of including those pieces that convey its distinctive history and idiosyncratic character. From gowns by celebrated couturiers—including those from the wardrobes of exceptional women of style—to American sportswear, uniforms, hats, and shoes, this volume reveals the collection's eclectic and expansive range.

The publication of this book coincides with this spring's simultaneous exhibitions drawn from the Brooklyn collection: "American High Style: Fashioning a National Collection," at the Brooklyn Museum, and "American Woman: Fashioning a National Identity," at The Metropolitan Museum of Art. As curator of the exhibition in Brooklyn, Reeder has made legible the distinctive character of the collection through her judicious assembling of its most representative works, some of which have never before been exhibited. Andrew Bolton, Curator in The Costume Institute and the curator of the exhibition at the Metropolitan, has structured a conceptual framework around archetypes of American femininity during the period 1890 to 1940, integrating ensembles from the Brooklyn collection with supporting examples from The Costume Institute. In this way, Reeder's vivid survey of the Brooklyn collection introduces the public to its strengths, while Bolton's interpretive approach conveys the enhancement of its merits through this merger with the Metropolitan's holdings.

The exhibition at the Metropolitan Museum has been underwritten by Gap. We are especially grateful to them for their extraordinary support and participation in this historic enterprise. As in many past years, the exhibition and the efforts of The Costume Institute have benefited from generous contributions by Condé Nast, to whom we extend our ongoing gratitude. Perhaps most important, we thank the Trustees of the Brooklyn Museum and our colleagues there who had the vision to initiate the outstanding partnership that is inaugurated by the publication of this volume.

Thomas P. Campbell
Director, The Metropolitan Museum of Art

For more than a century, the Brooklyn Museum collected fashionable costumes, preserving this most ephemeral art form and making it available as inspiration for designers, as evidence for historians, and as a source of information and pleasure for the public. The costumes were always a favorite destination when I visited the Brooklyn Museum as a child. Magnetic, evocative, and magical, they had the power to fire the imagination.

By 1997, when I came to the Brooklyn Museum as director, however, I was disheartened to see just how significant the challenges presented by this collection had become. Costumes are especially demanding in terms of storage, conservation, and display, and their sensitivity to light means that there is no such thing as a permanent installation. The necessary investment in staff, money, and time required to utilize the collection as we would have liked, together with our ever-rising standards regarding the care and display of fashion material, meant that the Brooklyn's ability to actively use the collection was greatly reduced. More and more, this great collection was left in storage, despite our hopes and best efforts. In a city that is one of the world capitals of fashion, this was tragic.

As much as I was committed to the effective use of Brooklyn's costume collection, I was also dedicated to the concept of collection sharing among museums. The resources of the museum community are spread too thin for us to duplicate needlessly one another's efforts, and our collective holdings best benefit the public and scholars alike when they are used most efficiently. With this in mind, together with the Trustees and staff of the Brooklyn Museum, I began to explore innovative ways in which this historic and exceptional collection could be useful to the greatest degree possible. Stewardship and access were paramount among our concerns, not accumulation or ownership. The ultimate result was a collaboration with The Metropolitan Museum of Art in which the Brooklyn Museum has contributed a world-class collection and the Metropolitan Museum, in turn, will provide care of the collection, as well as permanent access to it for Brooklyn's exhibition needs. The Brooklyn Museum collection, though now part of the larger collection of the Metropolitan's Costume Institute, will retain its separate identity. This book becomes the first document of its greatest treasures.

Establishing this innovative collaboration between the Brooklyn Museum and the Metropolitan Museum was a long process, and it required a major effort to inventory, catalog, and photograph the collection as a first step in considering its future. For support of that endeavor, I am enormously grateful to the Andrew W. Mellon Foundation for its progressive generosity, and especially to Angelica Rudenstine, Program Officer for Museums and Art Conservation, for her thoughtful counsel and steadfast support. For accomplishing this overwhelming task in the most professional manner possible, I thank Jan Reeder and the extraordinary team she assembled for this project. Kevin Stayton, Judith Frankfurt, and Ken Moser and their staffs at the Brooklyn Museum also made invaluable contributions to its success. I am particularly grateful to the Brooklyn Museum's Collections Committee, under the leadership of Barbara Vogelstein, and our board of Trustees and Norman Feinberg, our chair, for their careful consideration of all of the issues and for their courageous and forward-thinking decision. And finally, I would like to thank our colleagues at The Metropolitan Museum of Art, who have already been the best partners for whom we could have wished.

The Costume Collection has enjoyed an illustrious history at the Brooklyn Museum. This collaborative effort ensures a secure and equally distinguished future for this unique collection, allowing it to be preserved, interpreted, and exhibited to all members of the public—who are, in fact, the ultimate beneficiaries.

Arnold L. Lehman
Director, Brooklyn Museum

Introduction

The Brooklyn Museum costume collection was formed over the course of nearly one hundred years through the efforts of generations of museum personnel, donors, and benefactors. Composed of more than 24,000 items, dating from the seventeenth through the twentieth centuries, the collection is renowned for the diversity and richness of its holdings. For three and one-half years, between 2005 and 2009, a professionally trained staff of eleven—consisting of a collections manager, conservator, photographer, seven curatorial assistants and I—had the privilege, thanks to a generous grant from the Andrew W. Mellon Foundation, of recataloging, photographing, assessing, and researching every item held in this rich treasure. Using state of the art imaging, electronic, and database technology, we were able to document the collection in its entirety and in ways never before possible.

The objects taught us much about the cultures and lives of the people who owned them and about the wondrous variety of ways in which people have chosen to adorn themselves. This book is a record of that profoundly enriching journey.

The most striking fact that emerged during our process was the degree to which the Brooklyn Museum's dedication to servicing the design community, which culminated in the opening of the Edward C. Blum Design Lab in 1948, impacted the development of the collection.

One of the Brooklyn Museum's earliest and continuing missions was to provide a link between the art world and the industrial and design communities by giving access to the collection for study and inspiration. The intent was to amass as many objects as possible for

Madame Helene Lyolene teaching a course on draping at the Brooklyn Museum, 1941 or 1942. Brooklyn Museum Archives. Records of the Department of Costumes and Textiles: Design Lab. Madame Lyolene class 1941 or 1942.

Charles James (left) with his assistant, Kate Peil, and an unidentified man at The Brooklyn Museum, 1947. James's ribbon dressing gown (p. 162) hangs in the background. Brooklyn Museum Libraries

this purpose. It was not until the mid-twentieth century, when the dual purpose of collecting fashion for its aesthetic value, as well as for its value to the commercial design world, would develop.

Collecting began in earnest soon after Stewart Culin became the museum's first curator of ethnology in 1903. He embarked on an ambitious plan to build the museum's collections by conducting what were termed "expeditions" to other world cultures. Concentrating on Native American and Asian cultures in the early years, between 1920 and 1928 he went on eight expeditions through Eastern and Western Europe, focusing on traditional textiles and folk costumes. These acquisitions became the foundation of the museum's extensive European regional holdings, which were augmented in the ensuing years, most notably by the acquisition of the Shabelsky collection of Russian festive costumes and textiles in 1931.

Although fashionable clothing was not a priority in the early years,

accessories such as lace pieces, baby bonnets, and handbags were accepted. In 1903, the earliest recorded garment, an 1890 graduation dress belonging to a Brooklyn family, entered the collection. But the first important fashion acquisition, in 1926, was of twelve ensembles by legendary couturier Charles Frederick Worth. These were followed by two more large wardrobe gifts in 1929 and 1931, each containing important examples of French couture. During the 1930s, collecting continued to center on study examples, with a few significant pieces accumulated in the process, until 1940, when a somewhat more formalized approach to the collection led to increased discernment regarding acquisitions.

Actress Anna May Wong presenting her "dragon dress" (p. 217) to Robert Riley, curatorial advisor to the Design Lab, at the opening of the Michelle Murphy Room, October 1956. William G. Lord, president of Galey & Lord, textile manufacturers, and chairman of the Committee for the Edward C. Blum Design Lab, is at center. Publicity Photographers, Brooklyn, NY. All rights reserved

Elsa Schiaparelli (left) with her "1906 Doll" (p. 225) and Michelle Murphy, curatorial advisor to the Design Lab. Brooklyn Museum Archives. Records of the Department of Costumes and Textiles: Edward C. Blum Design Laboratory. Design Lab; Michelle Murphy and Elsa Schiaparelli (1949–54)

Along with collecting materials for study, the museum fulfilled its mission to assist industry through a series of departmental entities that made object access and advisory and research services available to students and professionals. The first was the Textile Study Room, which opened in 1918. The Study Room gave access through small rotating exhibitions, on-site review with consulting staff, and a lending program. While such services, once established, continued to be offered by the museum from then on, the need for them peaked in response to the interruption in the flow of design inspiration from Europe during and in the aftermath of the two world wars.

In 1939, paralleling the outbreak of World War II in Europe, a second incarnation, the Industrial Division, was established. More formally structured with a designated curator and a dues-paying membership program, the division expanded its advisory services and organized promotional and educational events such as fashion shows and large-scale exhibitions that traced current and historical design trends. The curator, Michelle Murphy, was an uncommonly dedicated and charismatic figure, who was the motivating force behind the success of the museum's design services between 1940 and her death in 1954. One of her greatest contributions was promoting Charles James's relationship with the museum beginning in 1944. It was at this time also that several American women designers became involved and began donating examples of their work. The success of the Industrial Division gave final impetus to a long-standing plan to establish a formal entity dedicated to the research and development of industrial design, focusing primarily on the textile and fashion industries.

Named for Edward C. Blum, a Brooklyn Museum trustee from 1912 to 1943, and president of the Brooklyn-based department store Abraham & Straus, the Design Lab was opened in 1948 through funding from Abraham & Straus and other commercial benefactors. It was a state of the art facility, housed in the museum, which included a reception area, offices, exhibition space, and eight soundproof workrooms furnished with drafting tables and scientific and industrial equipment. The promotional and consulting services started in the Industrial Division phase were intensified and expanded. Ideas for projects were brought in and treated as closely guarded secrets as they were being developed. In addition to her in-house consulting services, Murphy became a public spokesperson in the media and at industry-related forums. There were two membership categories, one for individual designers and another for companies, including major corporations such as Dupont, Jantzen, and the Tennessee Eastman Company.

The dynamic synergy established between the services offered by the Design Lab and the building of the costume collection gained momentum after the Lab's opening. As the museum's reputation for

Hans Reinhart. Gypsy Rose Lee wearing Charles James's "Swan" evening dress, at the March of Dimes annual fashion show held at the Waldorf-Astoria, 1955. A similar version is illustrated on page 184. © Bettmann/CORBIS

Austine Hearst wearing Charles James's first rendition of his "Four Leaf Clover" ball gown, 1953. An identical version is pictured on pages 182–83. © Bettmann/CORBIS

being an important center of fashion research, teaching, and display spread, private donors, designers, and industry-connected personnel were eager to contribute their objects not only to foster new designs but also to have them preserved for their aesthetic and historic qualities. Gifts, including most of the garments and accessories illustrated here, poured in for the next twenty years.

Beginning in the mid-1960s, the Design Lab, along with a several thousand items designated as study materials, was moved in stages to the newly built facility at the Fashion Institute of Technology, eventually slowing the rate of donations to the Brooklyn collection. However, an acquisitions fund established in the early 1980s provided for important purchases made in that decade.

The pieces illustrated in this book were culled from the nearly 4,000 selected during the Costume Documentation Project as highlights to be professionally dressed and photographed for web and print publication. Each was designated as a masterwork for its exceptional visual appeal, and one or more of the following criteria: as an expression of an important moment in fashion, and/or social, history; as a representation of the best of a particular designer's work; or as an exemplar of creativity and craftsmanship. The book is organized according to the primary areas of strength in the collection. There are other strong areas, to be sure, some of which are represented by objects in the "Rarities" chapter. I gratefully submit this publication as a document of Brooklyn's magnificent collection, the people who formed it, the dedicated work of the project team, and of so many other individuals who contributed to accomplishing the rewarding task of fully evaluating it.

Historical Fashions 1760s–1890s

The essence of fashion is change. At the heart of its inherently fickle nature is the silhouette, the shape that is formed by the way the clothing relates to the body. It is the primary feature by which fashion's evolution is defined.

The examples from the eighteenth and nineteenth centuries illustrated here represent significant moments in that evolution. Each is an exemplar of the quintessential shape and fabric that defined fashion at the time it was made. The pieces dating from the 1860s onward overlap with the period in which the French couture was established, the focus of subsequent sections in this publication. Those presented here are fine examples from American dressmakers. Sports clothes from the 1890s, the decade when large numbers of women began to participate, are also included. Innovations in clothing forms, such as bifurcated skirts, were necessitated by vigorous physical activity. A departure from sanctioned dress codes in the 1890s, they gradually became part of mainstream fashion in the twentieth century.

Changes in silhouette are marked primarily by fluctuations in three areas: the position of the waistline in relation to the body's natural waist; the size, fit, and shape of sleeves; and the shape, length, and degree of fullness of the skirt. Throughout the eighteenth and most of the nineteenth century, the prevailing silhouette was achieved to a greater or lesser degree by a tight-fitting corset, which reconfigured the torso and bust, in combination with one of many variously shaped understructures worn around the waist to support the skirt.

While the side-hooped shape that was the dominant silhouette of the eighteenth century remained substantially the same with minor variations for more than sixty years, shifts in style began to accelerate about 1780. The proliferation of fashion periodicals, such as Nicholas I. W. C. von Heideloff's *Gallery of Fashion* (1794–1802), Pierre de la Mésangère's *Journal des Dames et des Modes* (1800–39), John Bell's *La Belle Assemblée* (1806–68), and Rudolph Ackermann's *Repository of Arts* (1809–29), ensured their rapid dissemination.

Fashion scholars attribute changes in nineteenth-century styles to diverse influences, including the courts of the First and Second French Empires (1803–15; 1852–70), the Romantic period in the arts and letters (1820–50), Queen Victoria's ascendance to the throne (1837), and Charles Frederick Worth's domination of the French textile and fashion industries (ca. 1872–95). While the influences did not always originate in France, how the French fashion industry, as the acknowledged leader, interpreted them became the mode for the rest of Europe and America.

As fashion historian James Laver notes: "It seems to be one of the principles of fashion that once an exaggeration has been decided upon it becomes ever more exaggerated."[1] The earliest part of the nineteenth century saw exaggeration not as much in the garments' shapes as in the extreme sheerness and impracticality of the fine white cotton from which they were made. For the rest of the century, sleeves and skirts were the focus of fashion's propensity for the extreme. The small puffed sleeves of the early 1820s ballooned out in the 1830s to winglike forms known as *gigot* (or the less lyrical English translation, "leg-o'-mutton"), so voluminous that they required extra interior pads for supports; the modest dome-shaped skirt of the 1840s grew to hazardous dimensions by the mid-1860s; and the skin-tight sleeves of the 1880s developed shoulder peaks in 1890 that rapidly expanded into the second incarnation of the outsized leg-o'-mutton in the 1890s.

The holdings in the Brooklyn Museum collection represent three centuries of European and American fashions. The earliest garments date from the second quarter of the eighteenth century and the latest from the 1990s. The museum began collecting fashion in the mid-1920s, long after the sixteen historical masterworks in this section were produced. Preserved in private hands, some for more than one hundred years, their acquisition says as much about what people considered valuable enough to keep as about the concerted efforts of the museum's professional staff to obtain noteworthy examples documenting significant fashion changes from the eighteenth century onward. The pieces were acquired in every decade from the 1930s to the 1980s, some as parts of large estate donations, some as standouts in smaller groups, and others alone. Four were astute purchases made by the curatorial staff from 1956 to 1983 to fill voids or to increase the depth of existing holdings in the collection.

French

Dress (Robe à la Française), 1760–70

Blue figured silk taffeta with brocaded polychrome floral sprigs
Brooklyn Museum Costume Collection at The Metropolitan Museum of Art, Gift of the Brooklyn Museum, 2009; H. Randolph Lever Fund, 1966 (2009.300.903a, b)

Composed of an open overdress with full-length box pleats at back and a petticoat revealed in the front, the *robe à la française* and the closely related variation, the *robe à l'anglaise*, were worn over side hoops (panniers) that created the skirt's quasi-rectangular form. As this imposing silhouette remained essentially the same from the 1720s to about 1780, fashion change was indicated by the evolution of textile design and decoration rather than by shape. The wide expanse over the hoops and the graceful unbroken fall of the back pleats afforded maximum expanse to showcase the luxurious textiles, which were an integral part of the elegant Rococo artistic and decorative scheme. Flowers were the dominant motif, evolving from the fantastic to the naturalistic in endlessly creative patterns that varied in density, alignment, and secondary design elements. The magic of this textile is in the play between the brightly colored floral sprigs appearing to be randomly strewn over the surface and the subtle self-pattern of meandering lacelike plumes dancing around them. Designed in two configurations, the floral sprigs are woven in mirror images and in different colorways to intensify vitality and a naturalistic impression.

British

Evening Dress, 1797–99

Alternating plain and satin weave silk stripes with blue, black, gold, and green warp print patterning Brooklyn Museum Costume Collection at The Metropolitan Museum of Art, Gift of the Brooklyn Museum, 2009; Purchase, Designated Purchase Fund, 1983 (2009.300.2198a, b)

The period of the French Revolution brought about radical changes in dress that were adopted in France and abroad. In the 1790s a high-waisted style fashioned in light-weight materials and requiring minimal understructure developed as a sartorial expression of revolutionary ideals of liberty and equality. Textile patterns also changed, in a dramatic shift from the ornate Rococo flowers and curves associated with the court to orderly stripes, sometimes aug-mented by small geometric or abstract pat-terns as seen here. Many of the pre-1800 examples of the classically inspired style such as this dress retained the two-piece open robe and petticoat format of the *robe à la française,* which was abandoned at the close of the century.

French

Evening Dress, 1809

White cotton mull with overall tambour embroidery;
star flower motif
Brooklyn Museum Costume Collection at The
Metropolitan Museum of Art, Gift of the Brooklyn
Museum, 2009; Gift of Theodora Wilbour, 1947
(2009.300.1806)

The vogue for dresses with under-the-bust
waists spanned the years from 1790 to about
1820, the period covering the French Revolution and the First Empire under Napoleon
(1804–15). By 1800 sheer white cotton dresses
modeled after the high-waisted columnar
silhouettes of the Greek chiton and other
draped forms of classical attire were adopted
for day and evening wear. For its sheerness
and fluid drape, fine cotton mull imported
from India was the most highly valued. The
style was encouraged by Napoleon, who
sought to identify himself with the structure,
power, and glory of the Roman Empire.

American

Wedding Ensemble, 1808

Khaki silk taffeta and satin; beige and tan silk
taffeta; cream plain weave cotton; cream
organdy
Brooklyn Museum Costume Collection at The
Metropolitan Museum of Art, Gift of the
Brooklyn Museum, 2009; Gift of Helen Stevens
Wright, 1945 (2009.300.1436a–g)

Rare for both its early date and com-
pleteness, this seven-piece wedding
ensemble evinces the refined simplicity
and exquisite workmanship for which
the Quaker culture is renowned. It is
composed of an Empire-waisted taffeta
gown, coordinating satin and taffeta
stole, organdy fichu, satin bonnet with
a cotton underbonnet, spangled silk
brisé fan, and satin slippers. The subtle
manipulation of light from reflective
variations in the satin and taffeta and
the contrasting facings on the stole and
bonnet ties testify to the Quakers' art.

American

Evening Dress, ca. 1820

Lavender silk gauze woven with mauve ombré twill stripes; mauve silk satin trim
Brooklyn Museum Costume Collection at The Metropolitan Museum of Art,
Gift of the Brooklyn Museum, 2009 (2009.300.44)

At no time in the history of fashion does style express the artistic
mood of a period more than the Romantic era between 1820 and
1850. After the fall of the First French Empire under Napoleon,
the spare white cotton Hellenic styles of that epoch evolved into
more elaborate forms that reflected the Romantics' sentimental
yearning for the past. Details of historic dress, such as puffs
emerging from slashed effects on sleeves and wider skirts weighted
by elaborate hem decorations, were typical. A transitional piece,
this dress retains a popular bodice decoration of the Napoleonic
period that interprets the braid and button trim on uniforms worn
by the hussars, regiments of light cavalry who fought for France.

American

Dress, 1832–35

Natural plain weave dyed cotton
Brooklyn Museum Costume Collection at The
Metropolitan Museum of Art, Gift of the
Brooklyn Museum, 2009; H. Randolph Lever
Fund, 1971 (2009.300.948a–c)

The sleeve puffs of the 1820s developed
into full-blown balloon shapes, known
as *gigot* in French for their resemblance
to the shape of a mutton leg. Corresponding to the poetic aesthetic of the Romantic
age, and belying the actual discomfort
of wearing them, the dresses with their
enormous yet graceful sleeves gave
women a fairylike appearance. Curatorial notes written at the time this dress
was purchased affirm its desirability for
the collection based on the vibrancy and
visual impact of the fabric. By the 1830s
many advances had been made in textile
printing techniques, which increased
creativity and productivity and led to a
fashion for printed cotton dresses need-
ing no further adornment beyond their
vibrant printed designs. The light part of
this pattern is free of dye, indicating that
a resist or discharge dye process was
used. Mechanized ways for accomplishing this technique had been established
by this period.

American

Evening or Wedding Dress,
1840–42

Ivory silk satin
Brooklyn Museum Costume Collection
at The Metropolitan Museum of Art,
Gift of the Brooklyn Museum, 2009;
Gift of Claire Lorraine Wilson, 1942
(2009.300.668)

The fashions of the 1840s were, compared with the flamboyance of the Romantic period, demure and constrained, in keeping with the conservative influence of Queen Victoria, who was crowned in 1837 and married in a dress resembling this style in 1840. The silhouette, perfectly captured in this sumptuous example, featured a tightly fitted tubular bodice with an elongated, pointed waist atop a full, symmetrically gathered dome-shaped skirt. Not altogether modest, the shape emphasized the bust and minimized the size of the waist. The fine cartridge pleating gathering the skirt at the waist is exceptionally well executed.

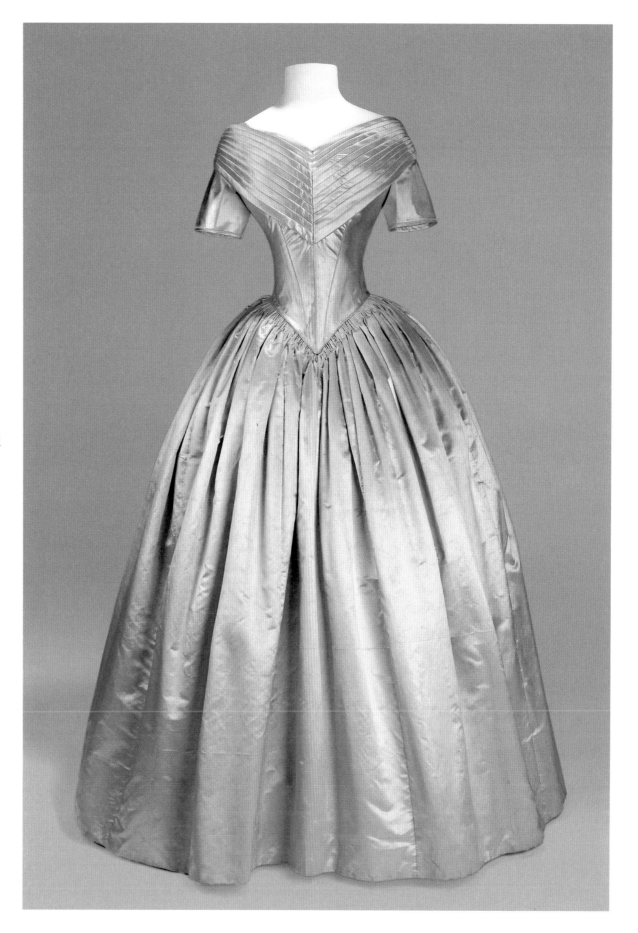

American

Evening Dress, 1858–59

Brown and white silk compound weave
Brooklyn Museum Costume Collection at The
Metropolitan Museum of Art, Gift of the
Brooklyn Museum, 2009; Gift of the Jason and
Peggy Westerfield Collection, 1969 (2009.300.922)

Skirts gradually increased in fullness and
waists rose to a more natural position in
the 1850s. Tiered skirts typified the decade's
style. Fabrics for tiers were woven *à la
disposition*, meaning that the design was
configured specifically to the shape of the
pattern piece for which it was intended.
Here the stripes were woven into the
fabric at intervals long enough to accommodate the full length of a skirt, so that
they would appear only at the hem. For
the tier the fabric would have been cut
midway between the stripe intervals to
create the proper length. The geometric
textile pattern is a striking counterpoint
to the curvaceous lines of the dress.

American

Afternoon Dress, ca. 1865

Red silk faille; red and cream silk satin ribbon; gilt metal
Brooklyn Museum Costume Collection at The Metropolitan Museum of
Art, Gift of the Brooklyn Museum, 2009; Gift of Dr. and Mrs. Edward N.
Goldstein, 1983 (2009.300.1000a, b)

As skirts grew in circumference from the 1840s, the weight of
increased layers of petticoats added significantly to discomfort.
In 1856 the need for petticoat layers was obviated by the inven-
tion of the cage crinoline, an understructure composed of
lightweight concentric hoops that could be produced in any
size or shape. Over the next decade skirts inevitably expanded
to the point of impracticality, reaching their apogee about the
time this dress was made. The unusually specific military-
inspired decorations of the dress suggest that it may have been
made for a patriotic event related to the Civil War. The vivid
red color, another outstanding feature, would have been achieved
by using aniline dyes, synthetics first put into use in 1858.

American

Walking Dress, 1870–75

Taupe silk taffeta and satin; black machine-made lace
Brooklyn Museum Costume Collection at The Metropolitan
Museum of Art, Gift of the Brooklyn Museum, 2009; Purchase,
Dick S. Ramsay Fund, 1956 (2009.300.1900a–c)

The bustle, perhaps Victorian fashion's most peculiar
form, appeared in two incarnations, the first about
1867. It was devised as a way to manage the copious
amounts of material used in crinoline skirts. A descen-
dant of the small back rolls common in earlier period
styles and the puffed polonaise dresses of the late eighteenth century, the 1860s bustle originated with the
idea of tying up the fabric at back for walking. As the
shape became the new fashion, ensembles were formally constructed with back drapes and puffs supported by interior understructures. Typical for the
period, this dress is composed of a bodice and two
skirts—a floor-length pleated and shirred underskirt
and a knee-length apron-front overskirt with double
puffs and pointed panels at back. The ruched oblong
pocket at right back side serves a practical as well as
decorative purpose. Previous museum scholarship
identified this as a probable early ready-to-wear design.
It is a style that would have been worn for visiting or
an afternoon outing.

American

Afternoon Ensemble, 1885–88

Royal blue silk satin; blue silk satin brocaded
with polychrome and gold metallic floral
motifs; blue chenille fringe
Brooklyn Museum Costume Collection at The
Metropolitan Museum of Art, Gift of the
Brooklyn Museum, 2009; Gift of Cornelia
Beall, 1963 (2009.300.2033a–e)

The second bustle form, which originated in about 1883, was more structured and pronounced than the earlier
rounded and puffed version. Construction of the gowns was complicated and
asymmetrical. Like sculpture, each van-
tage point afforded the viewer a different visual experience. The skirt on this
example is gracefully draped and plain
on the left side, while the right side is
rigidly pleated and decorated with rectangular insertions of floral brocade. An
unusual feature is the dolman wrap,
constructed of the same brocade fabric
that forms the skirt and bodice.

R. H. White & Company

(American)

Evening Dress, 1885

Blue silk satin; white swansdown; cream uncut silk pile on blue satin ground; cream embroidered net lace; label: "R. H. White & Co./Boston"
Brooklyn Museum Costume Collection at The Metropolitan Museum of Art, Gift of the Brooklyn Museum, 2009; Gift of John R. Hotson, 1946 (2009.300.1803a, b)

Ice blue satin, lacelike patterns of cream velvet, and pure white swansdown evoke images of winter evening galas and rides in a horse-drawn sleigh, an impression reinforced by this dress's Boston origins. Its one-piece construction, narrow shape, and corsetlike bodice place it stylistically in the period between the two bustles—1876 to 1883—when skirts were tighter and bodices fit over the hips, sometimes configured as exterior corsets with front lace-ups, as on this example. Its documented association with a wedding in 1885 confirms the notion that Americans, most particularly Bostonians, were conservative in their reponse to changing silhouettes.

Mrs. Arnold
(American)

Dinner Dress, 1894–96

Black silk satin; black net lace; label: "Mrs. Arnold/169 Clinton St./B-klyn" Brooklyn Museum Costume Collection at The Metropolitan Museum of Art, Gift of the Brooklyn Museum, 2009; Gift of Sally Ingalls, 1932 (2009.300.643a, b)

The second version of the 1830s *gigot,* or leg-o'-mutton, sleeve was in vogue from the early years of the 1890s to 1896, when it reached maximum proportions. The decade's hourglass silhouette, featuring wide shoulders, a small natural waist, and a bell-shaped skirt, is perfectly captured in this gown of unadorned black satin. The design and cutting skills of Mrs. Arnold, a Brooklyn dressmaker, are evident in its unusually elegant line.

French

Beach Ensemble, 1895–1900

Black silk taffeta; cream cotton bobbin lace; black cotton
cambric; mother-of-pearl; white lace
Brooklyn Museum Costume Collection at The Metropolitan
Museum of Art, Gift of the Brooklyn Museum, 2009; Gift of
Mrs. Frederick H. Prince, Jr., 1967 (2009.300.1331a–e)

High style at the beach characterizes this dress and
bloomer ensemble. Made of delicate silk taffeta that
would be ruined by seawater, it was meant to be worn
at fashionable seaside outings, but not for swimming.
The ensemble features a middy collar and tie, a popular
style taken from sailors' uniforms, paired with unlikely
feminine touches—a white lace dickey, mother-of-
pearl buttons, and an apron-tied bow at the back
waist. A multiruffled nineteenth-century style- cotton
bonnet or a wrapped scarf are alternative protections
from the sun.

Probably American

Sweater, ca. 1895

Cream wool knit
Brooklyn Museum Costume Collection at
The Metropolitan Museum of Art, Gift of
the Brooklyn Museum, 2009; Gift of Mrs.
John Hubbard, 1938 (2009.300.1111)

Style and function converge in this
rare ribbed knit sweater crafted
with three different patterns that
shape it, a fold-over turtleneck
collar—more associated with the
1970s than the 1890s—and fashionable leg-o'-mutton sleeves. It was
probably worn for sporting activities. Early casual wear is rare in
museum collections because of the
frequent use it received and the
greater value placed on more formal
attire.

American

Riding Ensemble, ca. 1896

Ivory wool broadcloth; tan suede leather;
cream cotton with windowpane plaid
Brooklyn Museum Costume Collection at
The Metropolitan Museum of Art, Gift
of the Brooklyn Museum, 2009; Gift of
the Princess Viggo in accordance with the
wishes of the Misses Hewitt, 1931
(2009.300.640a–g)

While nineteenth-century riding
habits with matching wool jackets
and skirts—proper attire for horse
shows or organized hunts—are
common in museum collections,
this less conventional ensemble that
includes pants gives a rare glimpse
of alternative attire for riding in less
regimented circumstances. It was
owned by Eleanor Hewitt, an
accomplished horsewoman, who
rode on the grounds of her home,
"Ringwood Manor," in northern
New Jersey. The ensemble comprises
a fashionably tailored jacket, several
interchangeable man-tailored wool
vests, a mid-calf-length suede skirt,
two pairs of suede jodhpurs, and
knee-high gaiters. The skirt, while
flat at front, has multiple side and
back pleats that give volume where
it is needed for sitting the horse
astride rather than sidesaddle.

In the 1890s women took up
bicycling in earnest, and for the
first time wearing bifurcated garments—most often under skirts,
and only for that activity—became
mainstream. While we cannot
know whether Hewitt always wore
the skirt and jodhpurs together
or sometimes as separate options,
the outfit is an example of how the
need for freedom of movement in
sports was a catalyst for change
in twentieth-century modes of
female dress.

The House of Worth 1860s–1930s (active 1858–1954)

In a letter to William H. Fox, the director of the Brooklyn Museum, dated April 20, 1926, Edith V. Gardiner, the donor of the first Worth gowns to enter the Brooklyn Museum collection, wrote: "It gives me great pleasure to offer to the Brooklyn Museum the series of French evening and carriage gowns owned and worn by my late sister, Mrs. William Alfred Perry. Mrs. Perry had put these gowns away with this object in view, realizing that they were of exceptional beauty and would, undoubtedly, be of value in the future."[1]

From early royal associations through nearly one hundred years and four generations of dedicated family leadership, the House of Worth, the first *maison de la couture*, is legendary in costume history. Its founder, Charles Frederick Worth (1825–1895), was a charismatic and artistically gifted Englishman, who moved to Paris early in his career. Using his astute business sense, he capitalized on mid-nineteenth-century technological innovations such as the transatlantic steamship and the sewing machine. He was a primary force in transforming the French fashion system from a series of independent dressmaking shops into a major international industry.

Worth founded his dressmaking establishment in Paris in 1858. Applying innovative organizational and procedural concepts to his business model, he established the blueprint for the future great French couture houses that flourished in the twentieth century. One of his most significant contributions was to change the perception of dressmaking from craft to art by raising technical and aesthetic standards and identifying himself as an artist with ultimate authority over all creative and technical processes. Paradoxically, in order to handle the volume of demand for his clothes as his custom business flourished, he devised the concept of using interchangeable pattern pieces that would become the foundation of ready-to-wear clothing production.

Worth's sumptuous clothes were the gold standard for a clientele of royals, aristocrats, and social elites in the last quarter of the nineteenth century. None were more devoted or numerous than the wives and daughters of the industrial tycoons building America during this time, the period known as the "Gilded Age." For them wearing Worth was the requisite sartorial signifier of their elite status and class.

While there were several other talented dressmakers operating in Paris from the 1870s, Worth in his commanding role was largely influential in determining the changing nineteenth-century silhouettes illustrated here. Motivated by economic and business realities, he designed these silhouettes, which required prodigious amounts of yardage, as much to support the French luxury textile industry based in Lyon as to satisfy fashion's inherently fickle nature.

Surely, the most outstanding features of Worth's garments are the luxury and sheer beauty of the textiles, which he often commissioned specifically from the Lyon manufactories. Exhibiting a refined sense of color and proportion, his artistry is evident in the balance he achieved integrating the textures and patterns of the textiles with the cut and surface decorations of the garment. When working with a single fabric, he maximized the impact of the pattern by matching up the motifs at the seams in a way that formed an expanded variant of the original design. Worth's talent for reinterpreting historical styles in textile patterns and cut was another significant hallmark of his work.

When Charles Frederick died in 1895, his two sons, Jean-Philippe and Gaston, who had been working with their father at the house from their early maturity, donned the Worth mantle—Jean-Philippe as designer and Gaston as business administrator. As a new fashion aesthetic, lighter in color as well as in substance, emerged, the house shared its once devoted customers with other couture houses that had reached equivalent stature. The family tradition continued through two successive generations, with Jean-Charles and Jacques in the 1920s and in the 1930s with Roger and Maurice, who headed the firm until 1954, when it merged with Paquin, which closed in 1956.

The Worth formula of using beautiful textiles in artful and refined combinations as the basis of design was carried on by all of Charles

Opposite: Detail (front), Charles Frederick Worth, *Evening Cloak*, 1889

Frederick's descendants. The continuity preserved the reputation of the Worth name, and the house retained a fashionable yet increasingly conservative group of well-to-do clients through the first decades of the twentieth century.[2]

The gowns referred to in Edith Gardiner's letter consisted of sixteen extravagant couture pieces, twelve of them from the House of Worth, dating from 1887 to 1905. They belonged to Emma Frink Perry (1848–1926), whose husband, William Alfred, was a member of the socially prominent Pierrepont family of Brooklyn. A *New York Times* article describing the 1926 donation recounted that Emma Perry bought a Worth creation every year she visited Paris.[3] As the letter about the gift indicates, she understood their importance, and, in the spirit of philanthropy, preserved them for the rest of her life, some for more than thirty years.

This gift represented not only the first Worths but also the first European fashions accepted by the Brooklyn Museum. Their accession was a defining moment in the history of the collection, when fashionable attire was considered of sufficient historic and artistic value to acquire and preserve.

In volume and quality the donation remains one of the two most significant of Worth costumes. The other was from the estates of Eleanor and Sarah Hewitt, highly accomplished sisters who, in 1897, founded what is now the Smithsonian Cooper-Hewitt National Design Museum in New York City. The sisters had associations with the founding fathers of the Brooklyn Museum collections, who began their work at approximately the same time.[4] The donation was made "in accordance with their wishes," soon after the death of Sarah in 1930, by their niece, Princess Viggo (née Eleanor M. Green), wife of Prince Viggo Christian of Denmark.[5] A sartorial document of their fascinating lives, it included twenty-two Worth ensembles, ranging from simple cotton daywear to elaborate evening wear. These two donations formed the core that attracted other Worth gifts. Over the next thirty-five years, some twenty-five donors gave an additional ninety pieces that dated from the 1880s to 1940. As if to underscore the enduring luster of the Worth name, the owner of the gowns dating to 1940, Elsie Whelan Goelet Clews (Mrs. Henry Clews, Jr.), wore the clothes of the avant-garde designer Paul Poiret in her youth in the 1920s but turned to the more conservative, yet still handsome, Worth designs in her later years.

Charles Frederick Worth
(French, born England, 1825–1895)

Evening Dress, 1862–65

Lavender silk taffeta; white silk satin and tulle; black velvet ribbon; label: "Worth & Bobergh/7.Rue de la Paix.7/Paris"
Brooklyn Museum Costume Collection at The Metropolitan Museum of Art, Gift of the Brooklyn Museum, 2009; Purchase, Designated Purchase Fund, 1987 (2009.300.1372a–d)

Worth opened his first business in partnership with Swedish businessman Otto Bobergh in 1858. At about the same time his designs caught the attention of Empress Eugénie. She soon commissioned Worth as exclusive dressmaker for attire worn at court. Scholars have noted that it was the simplicity of his designs relative to the overly frothy fashions of the period that attracted her. While he initially presented pared-down versions of the prevailing tulle-swathed aesthetic, less fussy monochromatic styles were the mode by the 1860s. Here the elegance of line and broad surface of shimmering taffeta is enhanced by petaled self-ruffles that add texture rather than contrast. Worth's refinement is evident in the white satin ruffle facing revealed only with movement. The dress has a bare ball bodice and a more modest one for day, pictured here. Garments with the Worth & Bobergh label are rare, as the partnership ended in 1870–71.

Attributed to François-Benjamin-Maria Delessert (French, 1817–1868). *Empress Eugénie and the Prince Imperial*, 1862. Albumen silver print from glass negative. The Metropolitan Museum of Art, Gilman Collection, Purchase, Gift of The Howard Gilman Foundation, by exchange, 2005 (2005.100.631). Empress Eugénie wears a dress similar to the Worth example illustrated here.

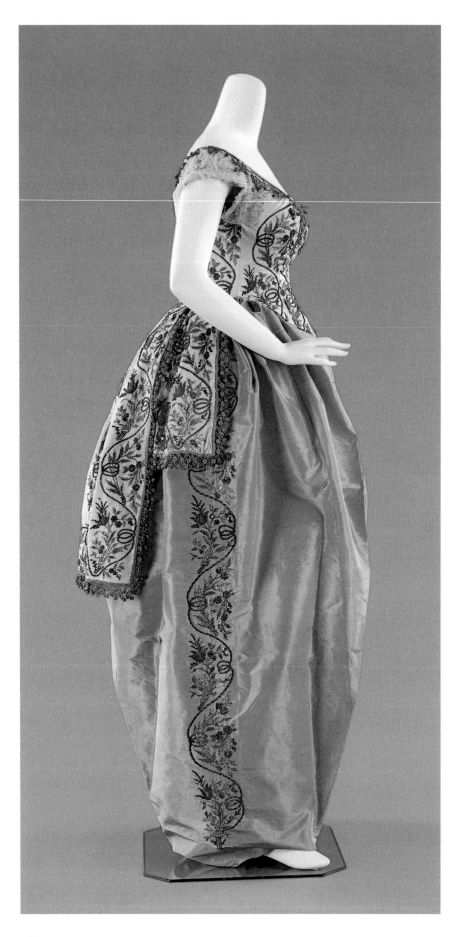

Charles Frederick Worth
(French, born England, 1825–1895)

Fancy Dress Costume, ca. 1870

Cream and blue silk taffeta; gold metallic and spangle embroidery, tulip and other floral motifs; gold crochet trim; label: "Worth/7 Rue de la Paix./Paris"
Brooklyn Museum Costume Collection at The Metropolitan Museum of Art, Gift of the Brooklyn Museum, 2009; Purchase, Designated Purchase Fund, 1983 (2009.300.1363a, b)

"Fancy dress" is the name ascribed to attire worn for elaborate costumed social affairs. From the early eighteenth-century masquerades held in public spaces in London and Paris to perfectly orchestrated nineteenth- and early twentieth-century A-list events, such as Paul Poiret's famed 1002nd Night Ball of 1911, costumes evoking what was then perceived as the exoticism of the East, especially Turkey, were a frequent theme of choice. With the pace and structure of social intercourse increasing by the third quarter of the nineteenth century, opportunities for such events proliferated. Invitees went to great lengths and expense in planning their costumes, the wealthiest commissioning the House of Worth to manifest their fantasies. A rarity among Worth fancy dress costumes, this is authentic traditional Turkish woman's attire, consisting of wide drawstring pants and a loose bodice, both heavily embroidered in gold by Turkish artisans. The pants remain in original form, but the bodice was refashioned, with careful attention to symmetrical placement of the embroidery design, into the form-fitting silhouette of the 1870s.

Afternoon Dress, ca. 1872

Purple silk satin; purple bengaline, chevron pattern; mother-of-pearl buttons; label: "Worth/7. Rue de la Paix./Paris"
Brooklyn Museum Costume Collection at The Metropolitan Museum of Art, Gift of the Brooklyn Museum, 2009; Gift of Alice Welles, 1933 (2009.300.1110a, b)

Two fabrics of the same rich color subtly varied in texture and tone combine to opulent effect in this afternoon dress. Chevron-patterned bengaline of a dark hue fashioning the sleeves and overdrapery is highlighted against the slightly lighter plain satin of the bodice and skirt. The beautifully crafted tassel fringes, each knotted at top and individually applied to edges of the drapery, are other refinements that speak of Worth artistry.

While rounded back protrusions are a familiar shape in fashion, the form first defined the silhouette in the 1860s, when stylish women dealt with what had become the excessive volume of their skirts by pulling them back into puffs to facilitate walking. Because this practice repositioned but did not lessen the amount of fabric used in crinoline styles, Worth, in his self-appointed role of patron to the French textile industry, championed this new trend, formalizing the shape with designs having various built-in supports. The puffed bustle prevailed for about seven years and was replaced by a tighter fitting silhouette in 1874. In the early 1880s Worth sought once again to stimulate textile sales by reinstituting the bustle dress, this time as a more exaggerated form that was shelflike at its most extreme.

Although the bustle style may appear odd to modern eyes, its graceful sway when the wearer walked had a seductive connotation to the Victorians.

Charles Frederick Worth
(French, born England, 1825–1895)

Afternoon Dress, ca. 1875

Moss green silk faille; navy blue and gold compound weave, scale pattern; label: "Worth/7. Rue de la Paix/Paris" Brooklyn Museum Costume Collection at The Metropolitan Museum of Art, Gift of the Brooklyn Museum, 2009; Gift of the Princess Viggo in accordance with the wishes of the Misses Hewitt, 1931 (2009.300.1100a, b)

The unusual color combination and extraordinary patterned bodice fabric that cascades down the skirt back of the dress are its distinguishing features. Textile patterns such as this one with overlapping scallops, known as scale patterns, were part of the standard repertoire for Worth in the 1870s and 1880s. Yet the density and small size of this design and the textile's structural complexity suggest it may have been woven earlier in the century. Worth is known to have bought older unsold stock from the Lyon textile manufactories to incorporate into his models.

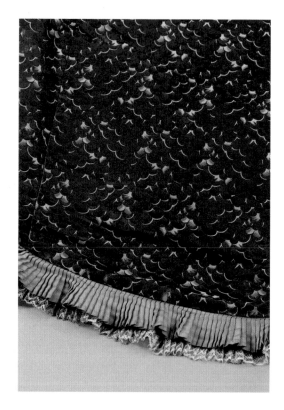

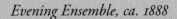

Evening Ensemble, ca. 1888

Marigold silk faille; cut and uncut silk velvet voided to cream silk satin, with rust, olive, beige, and tan lily bouquet motifs; citrine green silk satin; pink silk satin; cream net embroidered with pearl beads, gold studs, and seed beads; label: "Worth/Paris"
Formerly collection of Emma Frink Perry (Mrs. William Alfred Perry)
Brooklyn Museum Costume Collection at The Metropolitan Museum of Art, Gift of the Brooklyn Museum, 2009; Gift of Edith Gardiner, 1926 (2009.300.1093a–e)

Allusions to historic dress were a constant and important theme in Worth's designs. Here historicism and modernism are combined in equal measure. The modern aesthetic of the Arts and Crafts movement, at its height from the 1880s to 1900, informs the lily-patterned textile, while the pleated hip drapery alludes to the mantua, a late seventeenth-century form of dress with similar treatment at the hip. The overall silhouette is the quintessential example of the shelflike bustle as it is beginning slightly to recede prior to its more precipitous fall in the following year. The dress has a bare ball bodice and a more modest one for less formal occasions.

Charles Frederick Worth
(French, born England, 1825–1895)

Afternoon Dress, 1888

Brown silk figured faille, satin starburst pattern; beige silk satin; brown and gold metallic passementerie; bauble tassels; label: "Worth/Paris"
Brooklyn Museum Costume Collection at The Metropolitan Museum of Art, Gift of the Brooklyn Museum, 2009; Gift of Mrs. William E. S. Griswold, 1941 (2009.300.664a, b)

This two-piece dress is composed of a coatlike overdress with a fitted bodice and open skirt and a full skirt underneath. Single lengths of uncut fabric falling from the shoulders to the hem of the overdress account for its elegant lines. A Worth trademark, the edges of the fabric (selvages) of the open skirt are left exposed, rather than turned back, as was the norm in dressmaking (see detail). While most selvages are woven in studier yarns dissimilar in color, those on Worth's luxurious textiles were woven of the same color and quality. The exposed selvages served not only as a decorative device but also as a signifier of the high quality and expense of the custom fabrics.

Afternoon Dress, 1889

Mouse gray silk velvet; silver metal bobbin lace; pink panné velvet; cream machine-made lace; label: "Worth/Paris"
Formerly collection of Emma Frink Perry (Mrs. William Alfred Perry)
Brooklyn Museum Costume Collection at The Metropolitan Museum of Art, Gift of the Brooklyn Museum, 2009; Gift of Edith Gardiner, 1926 (2009.300.1681)

Said to have been named for Alexandra, princess of Wales (1844–1925)—the handsome and fashion-conscious queen-consort of King Edward VII of England—the princess line was introduced by Worth in the early 1870s, soon after the fall of the Second Empire. A departure from all previous styles, the one-piece princess line has no horizontal waist seam, resulting in a slimmer and more body-hugging line at the waist and upper hips. The princess line has persisted in fashion to the present. In a typical melding of innovation and historicism, Worth evokes the Italian Renaissance in the sleeve shape and metal-lace bolero with standaway collar, styles associated with the Medici family.

Charles Frederick Worth
(French, born England, 1825–1895)

or

Jean-Philippe Worth
(French, 1856–1926)

Evening Dress, 1893

Blue silk satin patterned with gold chrysanthemum petals; red silk velvet; ecru machine-made lace; beadwork and metallic passementerie; label: "Worth/Paris"
Formerly collection of Emma Frink Perry (Mrs. William Alfred Perry)
Brooklyn Museum Costume Collection at The Metropolitan Museum of Art, Gift of the Brooklyn Museum, 2009; Gift of Edith Gardiner, 1926 (2009.300.622a–c)

Japonism became a prevalent theme in fashion and the arts starting in the 1880s. Here individual petals of chrysanthemum, the flower that has symbolized the Japanese throne since the eighth century, are so expertly designed and woven as to capture the implicit pull of gravity as they fall through the air. In a first-rate amalgamation of the antique and the new, Worth chose the large puffed sleeves with tight-fitting arms typical of sixteenth-century high fashion as surrogates for the prevailing leg-o'-mutton style.

Jean-Philippe Worth
(French, 1856–1926)

Ball Gown, 1898

Ice blue silk satin patterned with yellow and cream butterfly motifs, rhinestone and sequin over-embroidery; ice blue mousseline de soie; seed bead, silver metallic, and rhinestone beadwork embroidery, scroll motif; artificial pink roses; black silk velvet; signature label: "Worth/Paris"
Formerly collection of Jane Norton Grew Morgan (Mrs. J. P. Morgan, Jr.)
Brooklyn Museum Costume Collection at The Metropolitan Museum of Art, Gift of the Brooklyn Museum, 2009; Gift of Mrs. Paul Pennoyer, 1965 (2009.300.1324a, b)

In Japanese iconography the butterfly is a symbol of young womanhood and marital happiness. Capturing the essence of youthful beauty, the pattern of this textile was woven to the specifications of the skirt, so that the butterflies could be arranged in an overall design planned for its shape and dimensions. Size graduation of the motifs establishes a depth of space, into which the glittering rhinestone-studded butterflies flutter upward and disappear.

Charles Frederick Worth
(French, born England, 1825–1895)

Evening Cloak, 1889

Black silk satin brocaded with parrot tulip bouquets; black machine-made Chantilly-style lace; metallic passementerie tassels; pink velvet; label: "Worth" Brooklyn Museum Costume Collection at The Metropolitan Museum of Art, Gift of the Brooklyn Museum, 2009; Gift of the Princess Viggo in accordance with the wishes of the Misses Hewitt, 1931 (2009.300.1708)

Entitled "Tulipes Hollandaises," this stunning textile was produced by the Lyon manufacturer A. M. Gourd & Cie for display at the Exposition Universelle of 1889, where it won the grand prize in the Lyonnaise textile section. With a three-foot pattern repeat, it is one of the most costly fabrics produced at that time and can be said to be among the last of the great silk masterpieces of the Victorian era. Worth's design for the garment respects the supremacy of the fabric. Constructed with minimal seaming, the loose fit allows for an uninterrupted vertical drape that maximizes the impact of the large repeat.

Jean-Philippe Worth
(French, 1856–1926)

Evening Coat, ca. 1900

Black velvet voided to cream satin, Tudor rose motif; plain black silk velvet; black machine-made Chantilly-style lace; cream and black mousseline de soie; black sequin embroidery; label: "Worth"
Brooklyn Museum Costume Collection at The Metropolitan Museum of Art, Gift of the Brooklyn Museum, 2009; Gift of Mrs. William E. S. Griswold, 1941 (2009.300.94)

Historical borrowings from sixteenth-century England constitute the decorative pattern and cut of this evening coat designed by Charles Frederick Worth's son. A long-stemmed variation of the Tudor rose, heraldic symbol of the Tudor family that ruled England throughout the century, is woven in black velvet against a cream satin ground. The design is repeated on the bodice and sleeves in black-on-black appliqués and again in sequins at the neck. The unfitted style, showcasing the textile, and the rufflike stand-up collar interpret outerwear worn at the time. In a House of Worth hallmark, the textile pieces are matched up at the back seam to form an enlarged variant of the pattern.

Evening Coat, 1901

Dark green silk velvet voided to satin, ribbon and floral garland motif; brown fur; dark green braid and crochet tassels
Formerly collection of Emma Frink Perry (Mrs. William Alfred Perry)
Brooklyn Museum Costume Collection at The Metropolitan Museum of Art, Gift of the Brooklyn Museum, 2009; Gift of Edith Gardiner, 1926 (2009.300.64)

Comparable to a negative image, the pattern of this grand textile gleams in satin from the depths of the velvet pile rather than in relief against a voided ground, which is more often the norm for patterned velvets. In a perfect union of planar and three-dimensional design, the coat is constructed of four lengths of fabric, which are joined to create a different pattern from each viewing perspective. By 1901 wraps of dark hues and weighty textiles like this one were quickly going out of fashion. Lighter-weight fabrics in pastel colors replaced them.

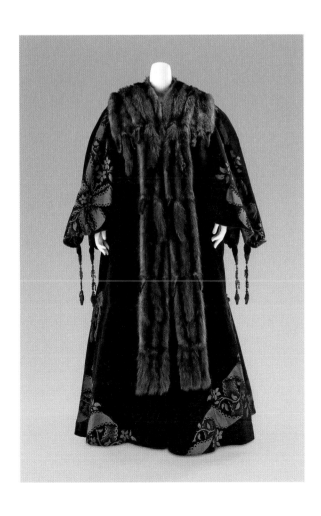

Jean-Philippe Worth
(French, 1856–1926)

Tea Gown, ca. 1905

Purple silk velvet; pink floss and gilt metallic
French knot and satin stitch embroidery;
pleated purple silk chiffon; black and cream silk
satin; label: "Worth/Paris/91437"
Formerly collection of Jane Norton Grew Morgan
(Mrs. J. P. Morgan, Jr.)
Brooklyn Museum Costume Collection at The
Metropolitan Museum of Art, Gift of the
Brooklyn Museum, 2009; Gift of Mrs. Paul
Pennoyer, 1965 (2009.300.377)

Tea gowns were garments that, less
structured and more comfortable than
streetwear, were suitable for entertaining at home. Elements of fantasy were
often incorporated into their design.
Here box pleats falling from shoulder
back into a graceful train recall the elegance of the eighteenth century. The
rich deep purple velvet, a typical Worth
textile, was slightly out of date by this
time, but chiffon and small-scale pastel
embroidery evidence the lighter sensibility of the Belle Époque, which is
generally considered to be the first years
of the twentieth century, ending at the
outbreak of World War I.

Evening Dress, 1907–10

Cream silk satin; cream net, rhinestone and pearl embroidery, lattice-work pattern; lavender silk chiffon; lavender crepe-back silk satin; black net, crystal bead and rhinestone embroidery; label: "Worth/Paris/94030" Brooklyn Museum Costume Collection at The Metropolitan Museum of Art, Gift of the Brooklyn Museum, 2009; Gift of Mrs. Frederick H. Prince, Jr., 1967 (2009.300.1334)

In silhouette and decoration, medieval high style is the design reference for this eloquent gown. Its allure lies in the contrast between the ornate eye-catching pearl and rhine-stone latticework of the tight-fitting bodice and the flowing unadorned layers of skirt drapery. Modernism has its place in the overskirt; two lengths of fabric are artfully draped from the bodice to hang in front and back points, with the selvages left visible.

Jean-Charles Worth
(French, 1881–1962)

Evening Dress, ca. 1925

Coral silk patterned with silver lamé, chinoiserie motifs; green and red seed beads; label: "Worth" Brooklyn Museum Costume Collection at The Metropolitan Museum of Art, Gift of the Brooklyn Museum, 2009; Gift of Mrs. Frederick H. Prince, Jr., 1967 (2009.300.2116)

Jean-Charles Worth, Charles Frederick's grandson, joined the House of Worth about 1910 and became chief designer after World War I, when his uncle Jean-Philippe retired. He transitioned the house style into a new era of simpler lines and silhouettes, but stayed true to the Worth design principle of promoting the textile. With this example, the fabric is expertly draped in a seemingly spontaneous gesture, but the careful placement of the border at the hem, which follows the shape of the textile, negates the possibility of any spontaneity.

Roger Worth
(French, born 1908)

Evening Dress, ca. 1938

Purple, fuchsia, and white silk taffeta
chiné, zigzag pattern; label: "Worth"
Brooklyn Museum Costume Collection at
The Metropolitan Museum of Art, Gift
of the Brooklyn Museum, 2009; Gift of
Ogden Goelet, Peter Goelet and Madison
Clews in memory of Mrs. Henry Clews,
1961 (2009.300.305)

The Worth family affinity for showcasing textiles still prevails in this
piece designed by Charles Frederick's
grandson, Roger. Cutting and fitting
the bodice, so that the bold paint-
erly design is transformed into an
alternate pattern, exemplifies the art
form that Charles Frederick perfected with the lavish textiles of the
1880s and 1890s. The blurred edges
of the zigzag motif result from
printing the design onto the warp
threads before the weaving begins.

French Couture 1880s–1980s

Clothes produced by the great French couture houses of the nineteenth and twentieth centuries represent the pinnacle of fashion's art. Because they traditionally have been the standard by which all other clothing is judged, costume curators prize them highly. Elements at the heart of couture clothing are innovative design, custom fitting, specialized handwork, attention to detail, and expensive, often custom-designed, materials. These imbue the end product with the distinctiveness, refinement, and perfection of line that are the distinguishing characteristics of a couture garment.

The term *haute couture* means, in its narrowest definition, "finest sewing," a descriptor of the technical virtuosity that is the essence of couture clothing. More broadly, it refers to the clothes themselves, as well as to the vast French fashion system organized around the individual couture houses that produce them. Today, although maintaining its original association, the word "couture" is used to refer to a wide range of higher-priced clothing and has lost its exclusive connotations.

The reputation for unparalleled quality that French materials and craftsmanship have earned dates to the reign of Louis XIV. Intent upon establishing France as the cultural center of the Western world, his minister of finance, Jean-Baptiste Colbert, made large investments of court resources in the French textile industry. At the same time he codified the work of the myriad trades that supported fashion production—embroiderers, weavers, dyers, furriers, makers of lace, ribbon, specialized thread, artificial flowers, and trims—in order to establish and maintain consistently high standards.[1]

The legacy endures to this day. Supported by the French government since the beginning of the twentieth century because of its value as an export, the couture business traditionally has spared no expense in experimenting with new silhouettes, colors, textiles, construction techniques, and decoration. Although greatly reduced in numbers, twenty-first-century couturiers still work with textile manufacturers and Paris's specialized ateliers to develop patterns and colors, trims and embroidery designs to be used by them exclusively.

Worth and several other smaller houses made up the couture industry between 1860 and 1890. Many more couture establishments opened in the period between 1890 and 1914, the number peaking to well over one hundred by the early 1950s. The French couturiers on these pages are some of the most successful of the late nineteenth and first half of the twentieth century. Each contributed significantly to the innovative ethos that drives their industry.

Jacques Doucet joined his father, Édouard, a contemporary of Charles Frederick Worth, in the dressmaking business in the mid-1870s. With his artistic eye, Jacques brought the house to prominence during the 1890s. He is credited with the first tailored walking suits in the 1880s, and the exquisitely decorated turn-of-the-century Doucet gowns are considered masterpieces of the Belle Époque (1900–1914) style.[2] Émile Pingat opened his establishment in the early 1860s. Next to Worth, he probably had the most American clients during the 1880s.[3] Since his output was small, surviving examples of his clothing are rare. Those that do exist, mostly outerwear, display Pingat's impeccable standards of workmanship. Some of his decorative motifs suggest a fascination with non-Western cultures.

Jeanne Paquin, Callot Soeurs, and Boué Soeurs established themselves as couturières in the 1890s. Paquin and her husband launched their house in 1891. Young and attractive, they rose to prominence by 1900, when fashion called for a more youthful look—light filmy fabrics, pastel colors, and elaborate inventive decorations. Perfectly suited for this sensibility, Paquin had a talent for creating ethereal effects by layering and blending fabrics and a keen sense of proportion and color. The House of Paquin was the largest and arguably the most influential in the years prior to World War I. The three Callot sisters opened their couture salon in 1895. Mme Marie Callot Gerber was head designer. They exhibited mastery in the use of lace and a great

Opposite: Detail (skirt), Jeanne Paquin, *Evening Dress*, Summer 1912

affinity for Asian construction and decoration. Boué Soeurs, a smaller house that opened in 1891, specialized in evening wear and luxurious lingerie and is especially known for ribbonwork.

Although Paul Poiret, Gabrielle ("Coco") Chanel, Madeleine Vionnet, and Jeanne Lanvin each established their couture businesses in the early twentieth century, their periods of influence varied. Poiret was most influential between 1908 and 1914, when he introduced a more modern silhouette based on the narrow high-waisted lines of classical dress and challenged the pastel palette of the Belle Époque by featuring brilliant saturated tones associated with the Orient. Chanel was next to forge a radical departure from convention in the 1920s, with her spare boy look for day and a minimal leg-revealing "little black dress" for cocktails and evening. She again made a major impact in the 1950s with exquisitely constructed suits and updated versions of her black dresses of the 1920s. Prominent throughout the 1920s and 1930s, Vionnet used her gift for mathematics and a lifelong fascination with fabric cut on the bias to create designs that related to the body's form. Tucking, wrapping, piecing, cutting, and draping distinguish her work. Lanvin started her career as a milliner in 1889 and designed children's clothing for a year before offering her first adult collection in 1909. By the 1920s her reputation was established, and her work remained influential throughout her long career. Her aesthetic was infused with romanticism but modernized with bold graphic decorations. The *robe de style*, based on the pannier shape of the eighteenth century, was a signature silhouette.

Cristobal Balenciaga, Alix Grès, and Jean Dessès opened their Paris houses in the late 1930s. Balenciaga, a Spaniard, became a Parisian couturier after closing his business in Madrid in 1935. Trained as a tailor, he is widely recognized as the undisputed master of cut, construction, and fit. Grès, who established her reputation with elegant draped and pleated columnar gowns based on Greek dress, later expanded her line with other innovative sculptural forms. Dessès, like Grès, was inspired by classical dress. His success was secured after World War II, when he was acclaimed for chiffon evening gowns with intricately pleated bodices topping multilayered flowing skirts.

In 1947 Christian Dior established his now legendary *maison de la couture* with a collection that rocked the postwar world through its full-blown romanticism rendered in extravagant amounts of what had been rationed fabric. Creating a new silhouette every six months, Dior went on to be the dominant voice in fashion for ten years until his death in 1957. Yves Saint Laurent took over as head designer at Dior for two years before opening his own business in 1961. Finally, Hubert de Givenchy, known for his classic styles featuring luxurious fabrics and elegant lines unbroken by pattern and ornamentation, became a couturier in 1952.

Most of the French couture items in the Brooklyn collection were given in small numbers. An exception is the outstanding 1967 donation by Virginia Mitchell Prince (Mrs. Frederick H. Prince, Jr.) of more than 300 high-quality costumes and accessories, ranging in date from the 1860s to the 1940s, that belonged to her, her mother, and mother-in-law. Virginia Mitchell's paternal great-grandfather founded Blairstown, New Jersey, in the mid-nineteenth century. She married into the Prince family in 1935. The Princes were owners of, among other properties, the legendary "Marble House," in Newport, Rhode Island, which the senior Mr. Prince purchased from Mrs. Oliver Hazard Perry Belmont (Alva Vanderbilt) in 1932. Virginia Prince's gift included twenty-two early couture pieces representing the work of many of the great early twentieth-century French designers. Most of them are thought to have belonged to her mother-in-law, Abigail Norman Prince.

Jeanne Paquin
(French, 1867–1936)

Ball Gown, 1895

Pink and white warp print silk taffeta, floral and meandering ribbon motifs; pink mousseline de soie; cream machine-embroidered net lace; artificial lilacs and roses; label: "Paquin/3 Rue de la Paix 3. Paris" Brooklyn Museum Costume Collection at The Metropolitan Museum of Art, Gift of the Brooklyn Museum, 2009; Gift of Mrs. Frederick H. Prince, Jr., 1967 (2009.300.2115a, b)

One of the earliest extant examples from the House of Paquin, which opened in 1892, this ball gown confirms Paquin's early reputation as a harbinger for the lighter, more youthful aesthetic that would characterize fashion from 1900 to 1914. Its rustling, featherweight taffeta with reductivist pastel pattern is a departure from the deep colors and heavier fabrics still in fashion but on the wane in 1895. Paquin's subtlety with tonal effects through veiling is apparent in the bodice, which is covered in pink chiffon in increasing density from front to back, gradually obscuring the pattern beneath. The skirt, on the other hand, is left unadorned, displaying the glorious textile to full advantage. The taste for historicism, however, did not wane with the change of palette. Here the exaggerated dimensions of the double-puffed sleeves and fichu-like lace overlay recall the fanciful dresses of the Romantic period.

Émile Pingat
(French, active 1860–1896)

Evening Cape, 1885–89

Blue silk velvet; black guipure lace; black
clipped ostrich feathers; red and blue plaid
silk; label: "Emile Pingat/30. Rue Louis le
Grand. 30/Paris"
Brooklyn Museum Costume Collection at
The Metropolitan Museum of Art, Gift of
the Brooklyn Museum, 2009; Gift of
Marion Litchfield, 1950 (2009.300.140)

Judging from their surviving wardrobes in various museum collections, Worth's American clients in
the 1880s and 1890s held Émile
Pingat in equally high esteem, especially for his distinctive outerwear.
Pingat's decorative aesthetic was
often marked by an unexpected
element. Here it is the plaid lining,
which adds a casual touch to the
formality of line, textile, and decoration of the exterior. The cape
encapsulates the wearer in a statu-
esque blue column constructed with
an opening at the back to accommodate the fashionable bustle.
Absence of arm openings emphasizes the wearer's status as a decorative presence in need of others to
attend to practicalities.

Evening Cape, ca. 1891

Cream wool broadcloth; brown fur; cream silk chenille fringe with beads; purple cord and brown knot embroidery; faceted stones; turquoise beads; label: "Emile Pingat/30. Rue Louis le Grand 30/Paris" Brooklyn Museum Costume Collection at The Metropolitan Museum of Art, Gift of the Brooklyn Museum, 2009; Gift of Marion Litchfield, 1950 (2009.300.141)

In an imaginative merger of cultures, Native American and French artistry intersect in this stunning wrap. The design, adapted from motifs associated with the Plains tribes of North America, is worked in French-knot embroidery, silk-cord work, and prong-set stones, traditional materials and techniques of the couture. The minuscule row of turquoise beads at the hem testifies to Pingat's superb eye for detail.

Jeanne Paquin
(French, 1867–1936)

Evening Dress, 1905–07

Pink silk tulle, mousseline de soie, and satin; peach silk velvet
appliqué, Greek key design; cream embroidered net lace; silver
metallic embroidery, laurel wreath design; label: "Paquin/Paris/
3. Rue de la Paix/London/39 Dover Street"
Brooklyn Museum Costume Collection at The Metropolitan
Museum of Art, Gift of the Brooklyn Museum, 2009; Gift of
Sarah G. Gardiner, 1941 (2009.300.1112)

Varying light-reflective qualities of silver, satin, and
velvet on gossamer tulle and chiffon produce subtly
shifting tones of light and color that epitomize
Paquin's artistry in creating ethereal effects. The
Empire-waisted silhouette and Neoclassical iconography—velvet Greek key motif at hem, laurel leaves
embroidered in silver, and repeat diamond motif in the
lace—reflect the Neoclassical Revival in architecture
of the period and, at the same time, presage the inherent classicism of Paul Poiret's revolutionary Hellenic
gowns of 1908. As hers was the leading house of couture during the Belle Époque, Paquin's promotion
of the raised waist would have been widely known
to the public, establishing the precedent for Poiret's
more radical designs.

Afternoon Ensemble, 1906–08

Lavender wool flannel; purple silk velvet; lavender charmeuse; cream machine-embroidered net lace; camel tan soutache braid; silk wound ball trim; label: "Paquin/Paris/3. Rue de la Paix/London/39. Dover Street"
Brooklyn Museum Costume Collection at The Metropolitan Museum of Art, Gift of the Brooklyn Museum, 2009; Gift of Mrs. Robert G. Olmsted and Constable MacCracken, 1969 (2009.300.1350a–c)

Paquin clothes were in their time recognized as the epitome of Belle Époque elegance and feminine grace. Finest-gauge fabrics, masterfully cut for optimal drape, and surfaces embellished with unusually complex interminglings of small-scale textural trims are two important aspects of Mme Paquin's distinctive aesthetic. The skirt of this ensemble, fashioned from the supplest of wool flannels, is simply cut in two lengths joined at front and back seams. In contrast, the bodice (see detail) is intricately decorated with high-sheen trims and textural laces that are designed to create subtly shifting effects of light and shadow against the matte simplicity of the skirt.

Jacques Doucet
(French, 1853–1929)

Afternoon Dress, ca. 1903

Raspberry pink cotton voile underlaid with cream silk taffeta; cream machine-embroidered net lace; pink taffeta bands embroidered in black and cream; pink taffeta; label: "Doucet/21. Rue de la Paix/Paris/66904" Brooklyn Museum Costume Collection at The Metropolitan Museum of Art, Gift of the Brooklyn Museum, 2009; Gift of Orme and R. Thornton Wilson in memory of Caroline Schermerhorn Astor Wilson, 1949 (2009.300.1153a, b)

The graceful S-curve silhouette, in fashion from the turn of the century until about 1908, is perfectly captured in this luscious raspberry-colored Doucet gown. It is typical of the style that would have been worn at garden parties or to the races, premier social events in France and America for sartorial display. The intricacy of couture workmanship is in evidence at knee level, where double layers of the fabric are backed with taffeta and manipulated into scallop forms with fan pleating and shirring at each interval.

Paul Poiret

(French, 1879–1944)

Evening Dress, 1910

Forest green and ivory striped silk; black silk chiffon; white pleated linen; brocaded ribbon; label: "Paul Poiret à Paris" Brooklyn Museum Costume Collection at The Metropolitan Museum of Art, Gift of the Brooklyn Museum, 2009; Gift of Ogden Goelet, Peter Goelet, and Madison Clews in memory of Mrs. Henry Clews, 1961 (2009.300.1289)

This is a rare example of one of Poiret's early revolutionary designs that were loosely based on the upright, columnar, high-waisted styles worn in ancient Greece. Requiring less restricting undergarments and conforming to a more natural body shape, they are regarded as a radical step toward establishing the greater freedom and comfort in dress that were to characterize fashion. One of Poiret's signature decorative techniques was to use folkloric textiles and trims that he collected in his travels. Here the collar and cuffs are fashioned from a traditional French pleated linen bonnet, while ribbons that would have adorned a festive folk bonnet encircle the raised waistline.

Jeanne Paquin
(French, 1867–1936)

Evening Dress, Summer 1912

Green silk faille stenciled with pink, brown, and green paint; cream cotton, chain stitch embroidery; canary yellow crepe; pink faille; label: "Paquin/Paris/3. Rue de la Paix/London/ 39. Dover Street/Été 1912"

Brooklyn Museum Costume Collection at The Metropolitan Museum of Art, Gift of the Brooklyn Museum, 2009; Gift of Mrs. Harry T. Peters, 1962 (2009.300.1294)

Worthy of being worn while cavorting with Marie Antoinette on the grounds of the Petit Trianon, this imaginative adaptation of the late eighteenth-century shepherdess style is an ingenious fusion of antique and modern, casual and formal. The cotton skirt front and bodice, adaptations of an apron and fichu, are embroidered with chain stitch, a modern version of tambour embroidery, while the green silk panel wrapping around the torso and forming two crisscross panels at back is a pared-down allusion to the puffed overskirt of a polonaise dress. A Rococo decorative design staple, the garland motif, is here stenciled in paint, alluding to eighteenth-century painted silks but abstracted in the contemporary aesthetic of the Arts and Crafts movement.

French

Evening Dress, 1909–11

Cream silk charmeuse; cream chiffon; silver bugle beads; turquoise and pearl tassels
Brooklyn Museum Costume Collection at The Metropolitan Museum of Art, Gift of the Brooklyn Museum, 2009; Gift of Mrs. Frederick H. Prince, Jr., 1967 (2009.300.1333a, b)

Although this dress is not labeled, the extraordinary beadwork embroidery signals its couture origins. In what constitutes a double trick of the eye, three-dimensional tassels are reiterated in fixed trompe l'oeil versions.

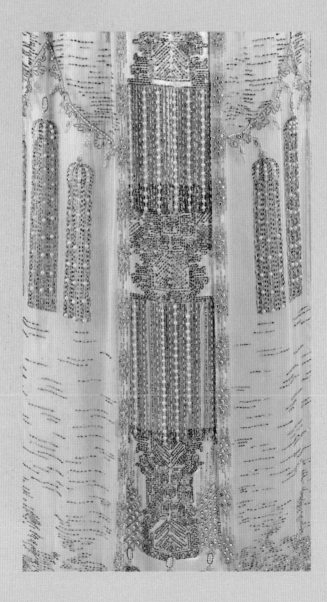

House of Drecoll

(Austrian, active 1894–1922; French, active 1902–1929) by Christoff von Drecoll (Austrian) or Besançon de Wagner (French, born Germany)

Dinner Dress, 1912–13

Black silk charmeuse; black net lace; ivory tulle appliquéd with chiffon floral and bow motifs; russet brown dyed squirrel; rhinestones; label: "Drecoll/Berlin"
Brooklyn Museum Costume Collection at The Metropolitan Museum of Art, Gift of the Brooklyn Museum, 2009; Gift of Mrs. Francis Lenygon, 1975 (2009.300.2611)

The silhouette with pannier side drapery was a new design in 1912. Combined with an attenuated pointed train and cutaway front hem, it represents the height of fashion for the period. Charles James reinterpreted this shape in his gowns from the late 1940s.

Callot Soeurs

(French, 1895–1937) by Marie Callot Gerber
(French, died 1927)

Evening Dress, 1914

Peach silk satin brocaded with silver, floral, and foliate
pattern; silver metallic lace; ivory silk tulle; label:
"Callot Soeurs/Paris/Marque & Modèle Déposée"
Brooklyn Museum Costume Collection at The
Metropolitan Museum of Art, Gift of the Brooklyn
Museum, 2009; Gift of the estate of Mrs. William H.
Crocker, 1954 (2009.300.1193)

The fashions of 1912 to 1914 were characterized
by asymmetry and implicit improvisation
that departed from the complex dressmaking
and tailoring techniques of former fashions.
Although it is not a single seamless length,
this dress has the appearance of having been
formed in one spontaneous gesture. Starting
from center front, the textile is wrapped
around the left side to the back, where it is
adroitly folded and draped into an asymmetrical shoulder drape in an allusion to eighteenth-
century styles. The wrapping continues around
the right side of the torso to end at left front,
where the exposed selvage underscores the pri-
macy of textile over cut. Meandering ribbons
in the textile pattern reinforce the historical
allusions of the back drapery. The buttons are
later additions.

Callot Soeurs
(French, 1895–1937) by Marie Callot Gerber
(French, died 1927)

Evening Vest, ca. 1913;
lace, Italian, 1650–1700

Patchwork of cream needle-made linen lace, gros
point de Venise type, two lace sources
Formerly collection of Rita de Acosta Lydig
Brooklyn Museum Costume Collection at The
Metropolitan Museum of Art, Gift of the Brooklyn
Museum, 2009; Gift of Mercedes de Acosta, 1954
(2009.300.1202)

Joining difficult-to-handle lace pieces and
shaping them into three-dimensional garments was a task that required the skilled
hands of the French couture.

Evening Dress, ca. 1913

Raspberry silk charmeuse and tassels; beige chiffon
Formerly collection of Rita de Acosta Lydig
Brooklyn Museum Costume Collection at The
Metropolitan Museum of Art, Gift of the Brooklyn
Museum, 2009; Gift of Mercedes de Acosta, 1954
(2009.300.1200)

Rita de Acosta Lydig (1880–1929) was a woman of singular beauty and grace who made a profound impression on the many early twentieth-century socially and artistically prominent figures who knew her. Her waist-length black hair, alabaster skin, turned-up nose, and famously long neck were the subject of scores of artistic works by such notables as Edward Steichen, Baron Adolf de Meyer, and Giovanni Boldini. Others wrote about the essence of her personality beyond her beauty. In the chapter devoted to her in his classic précis devoted to early twentieth-century style, "The Glass of Fashion" (1954), Cecil Beaton characterized her as a perfectionist devoted to the art of living who, through attending to every detail that touched her life, strove to be a work of art herself.

Lydig's wardrobe was an expression of her quest for artistic individuation. Her idiosyncratic style, best described as "bohemian," melded an old-world ambience with avant-garde daring. A passionate collector of seventeenth- and eighteenth-century laces, she commissioned the couture house Callot Soeurs, specialists in lace, to make up tunics, blouses, and bags using them. One of her most recognizable ensembles paired the tunics with one-piece bifurcated satin garments draped between the legs like the Indian dhoti, an adventurous and idiosyncratic look in the pre–World War I period.

The accessories on the following two pages are from Lydig's wardrobe.

Arnold Genthe (American, born Germany, 1869–1942). Rita Lydig, ca. 1910. Courtesy of Library of Congress, Arnold Genthe Collection

Sketch for evening ensemble by Callot Soeurs, 1913. Watercolor, pencil, and ink. Brooklyn Museum Libraries. Henri Bendel Fashion and Costume Sketch Collection. The design features a dhoti-style bifurcated skirt similar to those favored by Rita Lydig.

Callot Soeurs

(French, 1895–1937) by Marie Callot
Gerber (French, died 1927)

Evening Bag, 1910–15;
lace, Italian, 1650–1700

Cream needle-made linen lace, gros point de
Venise type; gold silk crepe de chine
Formerly collection of Rita de Acosta Lydig
Brooklyn Museum Costume Collection at
The Metropolitan Museum of Art, Gift of
the Brooklyn Museum, 2009; Gift of
Mercedes de Acosta, 1953 (2009.300.1852)

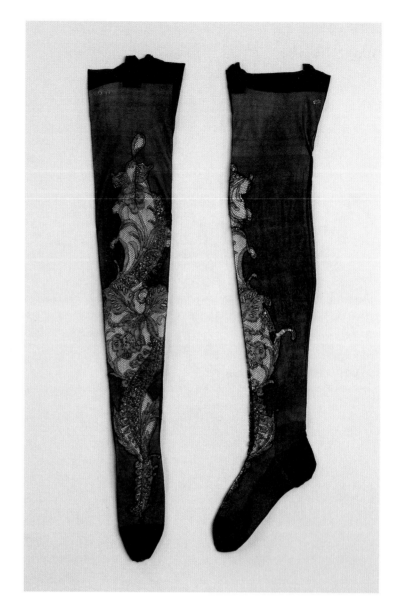

French

Stockings, 1900–1910

Black sheer tricot silk knit and lace
Formerly collection of Rita de Acosta Lydig
Brooklyn Museum Costume Collection at
The Metropolitan Museum of Art, Gift of
the Brooklyn Museum, 2009; Gift of
Mercedes de Acosta, 1955 (2009.300.1892a, b)

Seductive in the extreme, these custom silk stockings have silk ribbon
garter loops and are embroidered, as
were all of Lydig's underclothes, with
her given name, "Rita."

French

Chemise, 1920–28

White linen batiste; cream cotton bobbin tape lace, scrolling vine motif; white needle lace, stylized thistle and acanthus leaf motifs; shell pink silk satin ribbon; cream Valenciennes lace
Formerly collection of Rita de Acosta Lydig
Brooklyn Museum Costume Collection at The Metropolitan Museum of Art, Gift of the Brooklyn Museum, 2009; Gift of Mercedes de Acosta, 1953 (2009.300.1181)

Two types of handmade lace of undetermined date form the bodice of this chemise slip. The sheerness of the linen making up the lower part indicates its extremely fine quality. "Rita" is embroidered beneath the lace at left front.

Pietro Yantorny

(French, born Italy, 1874–1936)

Evening Shoes, 1914–19

Black silk satin; cream point de Venise lace; metal buckle set with square jet stones
Formerly collection of Rita de Acosta Lydig
Brooklyn Museum Costume Collection at The Metropolitan Museum of Art, Gift of the Brooklyn Museum, 2009; Gift of Mercedes de Acosta, 1953 (2009.300.1178a, b)

Yantorny was one of, if not the, most exclusive and expensive shoemakers in Paris during the early twentieth century. Working at 26 Place Vendôme from a private atelier, which he opened in 1908, he crafted handmade custom-fitted shoes for an elite clientele, whose ranks were limited by his exorbitant prices. More than two dozen pairs of Lydig's Yantorny shoes are extant, but she is thought to have owned several hundred. She most likely supplied the lace covering these shoes. Yantorny applied identical motifs to each shoe in precisely the same pattern, which would have required cutting out the pieces from a significantly larger piece of lace.

Jeanne Lanvin
(French, 1867–1946)

"Roseraie" Evening Dress, Summer 1923

White silk tulle, overall pink ombré ribbonwork embroidery; pink silk crepe de chine
Brooklyn Museum Costume Collection at The Metropolitan Museum of Art, Gift of the Brooklyn Museum, 2009; Anonymous gift, 1964
(2009.300.1318a, b)

A sartorial symbol of women's emancipation, the low-waisted tubular silhouette of the 1920s was a radical departure from the curvaceous shapes of the Victorian and Edwardian (or Belle Époque) eras. This dress epitomizes the boyish shape in the bodice but celebrates femininity with its extraordinary decoration and full gathered skirt. The ribbonwork design, in which flowers punctuate the intersections of a structured grid, is typical of Lanvin's distinctive decorative aesthetic, which frequently uses the discipline of geometry to impart a modern edge to her inherently romantic styles.

Evening Dress, Summer 1923

Silver lamé; red, pink, blue, green, and chartreuse ombré ribbon floral embroidery; blue satin; silver gauze; egret feather; label: "Jeanne Lanvin/Paris/Unis France/15/7/ Été 1923/51830"
Brooklyn Museum Costume Collection at The Metropolitan Museum of Art, Gift of the Brooklyn Museum, 2009; Designated Purchase Fund, 1988 (2009.300.2228a, b)

Lanvin's work is characterized by the deliberately sparse and well-balanced placement of decorative motifs. The embroidered motif on this dress is the pomegranate, symbol of fertility and a staple of woven and embroidered textile designs across cultures and centuries. Here it is executed with narrow ombré ribbon, a relatively new embroidery technique first used to embellish the fashions of the Belle Époque. Substituting for the more traditional glossy silk floss, it gives a textural modern edge to both the dress surface and the ancient motif. The looped train, a style promoted by both Callot Soeurs and Lanvin in the early 1920s, is a minimalist version of the Japanese obi. Lanvin made it her own by lining it with her signature "Lanvin blue," which, as Dean Merceron notes in his definitive work on the designer, she adapted from the frescoes of the fifteenth-century Florentine master Fra Angelico.

Callot Soeurs

(French, 1895–1937)

Wedding Ensemble, 1930

Headpiece: Madame Suzy
Oyster white silk satin; cream silk crepe de
chine; cream bobbin tape lace; cream tulle;
label: "Callot Soeurs/Paris/Nouvelle
Marque Déposée"
Brooklyn Museum Costume Collection
at The Metropolitan Museum of Art, Gift
of the Brooklyn Museum, 2009; Gift of
Mrs. Russell Davenport, 1963
(2009.300.1300a–f)

The influence of Asian and Islamic
designs featured prominently in
Callot Soeurs clothing. Evoking the
rippling waters of a Japanese land-
scape, the bias-cut cathedral-length
train of this otherwise quintessential example of 1930s glamour is
worked with a concentric scallop
pattern, adding definition and
character to the extravagance of its
dimensions.

J. Suzanne Talbot
(French)

Evening Dress, ca. 1925

Rust silk crepe with gold, silver, and white floral pattern; label: "J. Suzanne Talbot/ Couture Modes/10 Rue Royale.Paris.14 Rue Royale/Modèle Déposé/3555/Mme Prince"
Brooklyn Museum Costume Collection at The Metropolitan Museum of Art, Gift of the Brooklyn Museum, 2009; Gift of Mrs. Frederick H. Prince, Jr., 1967 (2009.300.2117a, b)

J. Suzanne Talbot, who established her couture business in 1920, was known as an original designer whose work was inspired by the arts of Oceania and Africa. In this most minimal of designs, she fashioned a single length of fabric into a simple one-sleeved tubular chemise and left the excess falling from the left shoulder to trail or drape togalike, according to the wearer's individual sense of style.

Boué Soeurs

(French, 1899–1933)

Court Presentation Dress (Robe de Style), 1932–34

Silver lamé; chartreuse silk chiffon; white tulle embroidered with
silver metallic, pastel ribbon work and rhinestones, flower-basket
and swag motifs
Brooklyn Museum Costume Collection at The Metropolitan Museum
of Art, Gift of the Brooklyn Museum, 2009; Gift of Aurora Elroy, 1957
(2009.300.1251a, b)

The low, wide-hipped silhouette, known as the *robe de style*,
was an adaptation of the pannier shape of eighteenth-
century fashionable attire, which Lanvin developed in the
early 1920s as a romantic alternative to the tubular boy
shape of the chemise dress. Other couturiers and dressmakers added the silhouette to their repertoires. While it
was at its height of popularity in the 1920s, Lanvin continued to show the style well into the 1930s. This spectacular
example by the Boué Soeurs was, according to Brooklyn
Museum records, worn at court in the early 1930s. The
type of ribbonwork embellishment, which entails manipulating silk or lamé ribbons into floral forms before applying
them to a garment, became synonymous with the Boué
Soeurs name because they used it liberally and executed it
with virtuosic perfection. The elaborate flower-basket motif
encrusted with rhinestones is repeated on the train back.

Jeanne Lanvin
(French, 1867–1946)

"Phèdre" Evening Dress, Fall 1933

Black silk crepe; channel-quilted silver lamé; label: "Mary Walls/Branch Shop/Waldorf-Astoria/South Lobby/East 45th St./New York"
Brooklyn Museum Costume Collection at The Metropolitan Museum of Art, Gift of the Brooklyn Museum, 2009; Gift of Mark Walsh, 1984 (2009.300.1365)

Aptly named for Euripides' (and later Jean Racine's) tragic queen, Phèdre, whose incestuous and unrequited passion for her stepson leads to personal and political mayhem, this slinky body- and skin-revealing black gown with flashes of silver lamé at the shoulders and double-pointed fish-tail train does justice to its namesake. In the January 1934 issue, *Harper's Bazaar* summed up its essence: "One of the most beautiful gowns that the mid-season collections brought forth is a Lanvin model called 'Phedre.' It is of black crepe Françoise, with long tight sleeves that forget themselves at the shoulders, and a seductive fish tail, which turns back at the corners to show silver lamé, sure sign of a Lanvin gown."

George Hoyningen-Huené (Russian, 1900–1968). Evening dresses by Jeanne Lanvin. *Vogue*, January 15, 1934, p. 23. George Hoyningen-Huené/Condé Nast Archive, © Condé Nast Publications

Harry Meerson (German, 1911–1991). Evening dress by Jeanne Lanvin. *Harper's Bazaar*, January 1934, p. 47. Courtesy of *Harper's Bazaar*, Hearst Communications, Inc. © 2010

Madeleine Vionnet

(French, 1876–1975)

Evening Ensemble, ca. 1935

Magenta and fuchsia silk crepe; label:
"Madeleine Vionnet/Déposée/95104"
Brooklyn Museum Costume Collection at
The Metropolitan Museum of Art, Gift of
the Brooklyn Museum, 2009; Gift of Mrs.
James Johnson Sweeney, 1968
(2009.300.459a–g)

In her modernist approach to dressmaking, Vionnet sought to create
garments that were in complete harmony with the natural line of the
body. To this end, she continually
experimented with the possibilities
of fabric cut on the bias, which
caused it to cling to the body and
fall with extra weight into graceful
folds. Decorative effects were integral with construction techniques,
obviating the need for external
trimmings. Bias-cut self ties and
panels that when wrapped conform
to the contours of the body exemplify this integral approach. The
bodice of this dress is constructed
with two panels that crisscross at
front and wrap around the waist to
a back buckle. The asymmetrically
cut evening wrap (frontispiece) has
an integral cowl collar and long ties
that similarly crisscross over the
front, then wrap around the waist
from back to front, where they
fall gracefully, seeming to merge
with the bias-cut folds of the full
skirt. The subtlety of tonal shifts
in jacket and bodice add to the
understated elegance.

Scarf, ca. 1935

White, light blue, royal blue, and black
silk crepe
Brooklyn Museum Costume Collection at
The Metropolitan Museum of Art, Gift of
the Brooklyn Museum, 2009; Gift of Mrs.
Edward G. Sparrow, 1969 (2009.300.2267)

Seagulls hover over a sailboat riding
on a restless sea. None but the most
skilled hands of the couture could
accomplish the exacting piecework
that renders this picturesque iconography. The impeccable geometry
of its forms speaks of Madeleine
Vionnet, known as the "Euclid of
Dressmaking" for her mathematical
approach to design.

Evening Dress (Robe de Style), ca. 1939

Black silk tulle; black silk velvet appliqués, stylized grape forms; label: "Madeleine Vionnet/Déposée/751[?]"
Brooklyn Museum Costume Collection at The Metropolitan Museum of Art, Gift of the Brooklyn Museum, 2009; Gift of Mrs. Edward G. Sparrow, 1969 (2009.300.466a–c)

After nearly a decade dominated by body-hugging bias-cut gowns, full-skirted romantic fashions were prominent in 1938 and 1939, in what can be seen as a nostalgic glance backward before the occupation of Paris and the onset of World War II. In this version of the *robe de style*, Vionnet used horsehair stiffening at the hips and a detached basket-shaped understructure (pannier) to create the hip amplitude of the tulle dress. True to her métier, the halter bodice is a simple gathering of tulle from the waist to a velvet neckband, from which it fans out into a shoulder covering. The separate sheath slip is bias cut with an integral halter-neck bodice that adheres precisely to the form of the dress.

Madame Alix Grès
(French, 1903–1993)

Evening Dress, 1937

White silk jersey; label: "Alix/Paris"
Brooklyn Museum Costume Collection at The
Metropolitan Museum of Art, Gift of the Brooklyn
Museum, 2009; Gift of Bettina Ballard, 1952
(2009.300.1174)

Madame Grès's career spanned five decades,
during which she created an incomparable
variety of styles and silhouettes in her constant exploration of the sculptural possibilities of draping fabric. She is best known for
her full-length classically inspired columnar
gowns fashioned through intricate pleating,
gathering, and draping techniques. As
described by Patricia Mears in her authoritative book on the designer, Grès's earliest
examples, like this one, were minimal con-
structions that showed a liberated creative
process. They were assembled by using two
lengths of fluid fabric that were sewn at the
selvages and ran continually, uncut, from
front hem, over the shoulders, to back hem.
Stitches at the waist defined the body. This
example has a front peplum, which is created by folding the drapery over itself and
sewing it at the waist. Side panels were
added to enhance the train. Grès would
continue to produce dresses in the Grecian
mode throughout the 1950s and 1960s.
They evolved into more structured compositions that employed a rigid boned bodice
as an armature, upon which the fabric was
manipulated into complex patterns before
cascading in voluminous folds to the floor.

Cristobal Balenciaga
(French, born Spain, 1895–1972)

Evening Dress, ca. 1945

White silk organza; black lace insertions;
flat black metallic sequins
Brooklyn Museum Costume Collection at
The Metropolitan Museum of Art, Gift of
the Brooklyn Museum, 2009; Gift of Mrs.
Russell Davenport, 1963 (2009.300.1299)

Balenciaga's work was imbued with
the aesthetics of traditional costume
and art from his native Spain. Here
he interprets the alternating horizontal bands typical of the skirts of
Castilian folk costume in sophisticated black lace and white silk
organdy bands. In an eloquent
articulation of other signature
design elements reflecting his patri-
mony, such as volumetric contrasts
and elaborate surface embellishment, he counters the minimalist
size of a fitted lingerie-style bodice
with a billowing multilayered skirt
and encrusts it with variegated flat
black sequins. The skillful dusting
of sequins, which diminishes in
density from top to bottom, is the
essence of couture sophistication
and artistry.

Christian Dior
(French, 1905–1957)

"Gruau" Evening Dress, Fall/Winter 1949–50

Ivory silk satin; label: "Christian Dior/Paris/06686"
Brooklyn Museum Costume Collection at The Metropolitan
Museum of Art, Gift of the Brooklyn Museum, 2009; Gift of Henry
Rogers Benjamin, 1965 (2009.300.2043a–c)

Perfectly proportioned and spaced buttons, self-covered or
unadorned, featured prominently in Dior day and evening designs of the late 1940s and early 1950s. Functional,
decorative, or both, they were used variously to emphasize
the garment's line and call to attention to the point of
accessibility to the body beneath. In this evening dress
their diagonal positioning accentuates the spiral effect of
the design, one that Dior would feature in his "Oblique"
line of the fall/winter collection of 1950–51. Similar in
construction to complicated early twentieth-century
bodices, this example has buttons that must be opened to
get to the hook-and-eye closure underneath. The skirt
buttons, on the other hand, are purely decorative, as a
zipper provides the necessary opening. This dress is suitably named for the French fashion illustrator René Gruau
(1909–2004), renowned for his ability to capture detail
and movement with an economy of line.

René Gruau (French, born Italy,
1909–2004). Evening dress by
Christian Dior. *Femina*,
October 1949, p. 71. © Éditions
P. LaFitte, Paris

René Gruau (French, born Italy,
1909–2004). Evening dress by
Christian Dior. Unidentified
French periodical, ca. 1949

Christian Dior

(French, 1905–1957)

"New-York" Coat, Fall/Winter 1950–51

Black pebbled wool; label: "Christian Dior/Paris/Made in France/12240"
Brooklyn Museum Costume Collection at The Metropolitan Museum
of Art, Gift of the Brooklyn Museum, 2009; Gift of Jeanne Eddy, 1961
(2009.300.299)

For each of his semiannual collections, Dior created a new
silhouette named for its source of inspiration. His "Oblique"
line, as the name suggests, was based on slanting lines and
spiraling effects. While the basic silhouette of this coat
adheres to the nipped-in waist and padded hips of his iconic
"Corolle" line introduced in 1947, the collar emphatically
interjects angularity into the equation. In its September
1950 issue, *Vogue* describes the form, which it dubbed "The
Oblique Collar," as a "beautiful arch of a collar, rolled
high, slanted from armhole to jutting point."

Jean Dessès
(French, born Egypt, 1904–1970)

Evening Ensemble, 1956

Coral and gold Lurex; mink; label: "Jean Dessès/17 Avenue Matignon/PARIS" Brooklyn Museum Costume Collection at The Metropolitan Museum of Art, Gift of the Brooklyn Museum, 2009; Gift of the Aluminum Company of America, 1957 (2009.300.810a, b)

Dessès mustered all of his acclaimed skill with pleating, gathering, and twisting chiffon to fashion this evening gown in Lurex, which is made with yarns fused with aluminum. It was invented in the 1950s as an improvement over lamé, the metallic fabric that, unlike Lurex, lost its luster to tarnish over time. Dessès made this dress for the Aluminum Company of America's (Alcoa) advertising campaign in 1956, presumably to illustrate the fabric's suppleness and pliability. A touch of mink underscores its legitimacy for the luxury market.

Yves Saint Laurent

(French, born Algeria, 1936–2008) for the House of Dior
(French, founded 1946)

"Refrain" Cocktail Dress, Spring/Summer 1958

White silk surah printed with gray and black pebble pattern; label:
"Christian Dior/Paris/Printemps-Été 1958/91916"
Brooklyn Museum Costume Collection at The Metropolitan Museum of
Art, Gift of the Brooklyn Museum, 2009; Gift of Mr. and Mrs. Lewis
Iselin, Jr., 1959 (2009.300.268)

Named for the apparatus from which acrobats propel themselves into the air, Yves Saint Laurent's "Trapeze" collection
featured dresses with fitted fronts and airborne backs that,
like the acrobat, appeared weightless and free of constraints.
Yet, like the acrobat to the trapeze, its liberated form is tethered
to the body by an understructure that makes the design possible. In this, his first collection for the House of Dior after
Christian Dior's sudden death in 1957, Saint Laurent elabo-
rated upon the looser lines that Dior had been promoting
in his last year, most notably the chemise—also known as
the "sack"—silhouette. Saint Laurent's design was greeted
with great acclaim for its modernity and youthfulness. Seen
in retrospect, it was an early harbinger of the 1960s youth-
oriented culture and a predecessor of the A-line silhouette
that typified fashions of the 1960s.

Henry Clarke (American,
1918–1996). Dress by
Yves Saint Laurent for
Christian Dior. *Vogue*,
March 15, 1958, p. 78.
Henry Clarke/Condé
Nast Archive, © Condé
Nast Publications

Hubert de Givenchy
(French, born 1927)

Evening Dress, 1960

Robin's-egg blue silk taffeta; label:
"Givenchy/Paris/Made in France"
Brooklyn Museum Costume Collection at
The Metropolitan Museum of Art, Gift of
the Brooklyn Museum, 2009; Gift of
Lauren Bacall, 1967 (2009.300.454)

Elegance and simplicity were the
essence of Givenchy's design philosophy. To fashion this ultimately
reductivist version of the *robe à la
française*, Givenchy employed a
fringed silk taffeta that might have
been purloined from the windows
of an eighteenth-century drawing
room. The loose fit, denying the
body shape in deference to the
sculptural drape of shimmering
silk, was an innovative silhouette
advancing the spirit of liberation
that would define the 1960s. An
integral bow fashioned by master-
ful manipulation of the fabric at
the left front bodice is a classic
couture flourish.

Cristobal Balenciaga

(French, born Spain, 1895–1972)

Cocktail Dress, Fall/Winter 1963

Black machine-embroidered nylon net lace; black plain weave silk; label: "Balenciaga/ 10, Avenue George V. Paris/Model 87247" Brooklyn Museum Costume Collection at The Metropolitan Museum of Art, Gift of the Brooklyn Museum, 2009; Gift of Mrs. Benjamin R. Kittredge, 1973 (2009.300.2176a–c)

By 1963 the fashion revolution dubbed the "Youthquake," which erupted in London in the late 1950s, challenged couturiers to show their modernity by interjecting a more youthful sensibility into their designs. Balenciaga adapted the traditional black lace and flamenco flounces of his native Spain to this semifitted flirty rendition of the classic black cocktail dress. While the lines of the lace overdress are more relaxed, standing slightly away from the body, 1950s structure is present in the strapless boned bodice of the slip beneath.

Gabrielle Chanel
(French, 1883–1971)

Cocktail Dress, ca. 1965

Black silk chiffon; wide black satin ribbon; black silk crepe de chine; black lace
Brooklyn Museum Costume Collection at The Metropolitan Museum of Art, Gift of the Brooklyn Museum, 2009; Gift of Jane Holzer, 1977 (2009.300.980a, b)

Chanel introduced what became known as "the little black dress" for evening wear in her 1926 collection. Spare and tubular, with a hemline ending just below the knee, it represented the epitome of her design philosophy, which championed comfort, function, and simplicity. As evening fashions lengthened and became more feminine in the 1930s, Chanel developed a romantic style that featured floor-length lace or tulle gowns embellished with overall horizontal tiers of ruffles often formed by a distinctive shirring at the top. The inherent femininity was, however, tempered by angularity of cut and a sense of underlying geometry in the decorative scheme. Forever the modernist, yet true to her original concepts, Chanel amalgamated the two earlier styles in the design of this dress. Here the 1930s shirred ruffles are disciplined by alternating heavy-gauge satin ribbons, and the back neckline is the regimented square of a sailor's middy collar. The amount of leg revealed by this 1960s length far surpasses that of its 1920s prototype.

Madame Alix Grès
(French, 1903–1993)

Evening Dress, 1969

Taupe silk paper taffeta; label: "Grès/1 rue de
la Paix-Paris"
Brooklyn Museum Costume Collection at
The Metropolitan Museum of Art, Gift of the
Brooklyn Museum, 2009; Gift of Mrs.
William Randolph Hearst, Jr., 1988
(2009.300.1373)

In an audacious juxtaposition of
linearity and volume, Grès displaced
her signature pleating and gathering
techniques from the body of the dress
to the sleeves. A simply sewn high-
waisted tubular dress is the support
structure for voluminous balloon
sleeves that push the boundaries of
technical skill and, of lesser consideration, practicality. As Patricia Mears
notes in her recent work on the
designer, Grès exploited the crisp light
qualities of paper taffeta to sculpt
billowing forms and poufs.

Dinner Dress, 1982

Iridescent silk organza; label: "Grès/Paris"
Brooklyn Museum Costume Collection
at The Metropolitan Museum of Art, Gift
of the Brooklyn Museum, 2009; Gift of
Mrs. William Randolph Hearst, Jr., 1988
(2009.300.1041a–c)

Departing from the classically
inspired and sculptural evening
gowns for which she is well known,
Grès designed a dress worthy of a
Degas ballerina. The balletic pose
and leotard-like bodice of the original croquis (fashion sketch) suggest
her intention in this regard. In her
translation, she replaces layers of
cream tulle with a multicolored
composition in organza. An over-
layer of black covers tiered layers of
blue, copper, and orange artfully
arranged to create an illusion of
iridescence backlit by an orange
glow, as if by the footlights on a
stage. The black neckband, a detail
often seen on Degas's dancers, is
interpreted here with multiple oversized organza bows.

Elsa Schiaparelli 1930s–1940s (active 1927–1954)

The Italian-born couturière Elsa Schiaparelli (1890–1973) is best known for the iconoclastic bravado and unrestrained, at times brazen, originality of her work. While her contemporaries Gabrielle Chanel and Madeleine Vionnet set the period's standards of taste and beauty in fashion design, Schiaparelli flouted convention in the pursuit of a more idiosyncratic style. As much an artist as a dress designer, she commandeered the talents of a host of prominent artisans and artists, most notably those associated with the Surrealist movement. Distilling their disquieting dream-based imagery and provocative concepts through her own creative process, she incorporated themes inspired by contemporaneous events, erotic fantasy, traditional and avant-garde art, and her own psyche in her designs. A repertoire of inventive devices—experimental fabrics with pronounced textures, bold prints with unorthodox imagery and colors, opulent embroideries, outsized and exposed zippers, and distinctive buttons and ornaments ranging from the whimsical to the bizarre—was her medium of creative expression.

Schiaparelli first captivated the worlds of European and American fashion with her inaugural collection of 1927, when she presented a sweater with an image of a knotted bow knit into the pattern at the neck, rendering in two dimensions what would normally be a three-dimensional decoration. Over the next several years, her offerings evolved from sweaters and sporting wear to a full line of clothing. These early designs, while more conservative than her later work, incorporated her quirky and imaginative aesthetic. However, the clothes that she created from the mid-1930s, when she was collaborating with Surrealist artists Jean Cocteau, Salvatore Dalí, and Leonor Fini, and enjoying continued inspiration from her long-term association with photographer Man Ray, represent the apotheosis of her creativity.

Further emphasizing the Surrealistic theatricality of the clothes from this period, Schiaparelli organized some of them into thematic collections—"Paris 1937" in 1937; "Zodiac," "Pagan," and "Circus" in 1938; "Music" and "Commedia dell' Arte" in 1939.

Prompted by security and business uncertainties precipitated by the war, Schiaparelli left Paris in 1941 and moved to New York, where, rather than designing, she involved herself with war-related volunteer activities. Her house remained open but collections were prepared by associates. She returned to Paris in 1945 after the occupation ended and continued designing until 1954. Her influence, however, was eclipsed by the emergence of a new generation of couturiers, most notably Christian Dior, who, in 1947, like Schiaparelli twenty years earlier, captivated America and Europe with what became known as the "New Look," which also had shock value but of a different, more demure, sort.

Because of their compelling visual and artistic qualities and relative scarcity, Schiaparelli designs are highly prized. The Brooklyn collection's extensive holdings of her works were formed primarily through the patronage of mid-twentieth-century arbiter of style, philanthropist, and artisan Millicent Rogers and her heirs. Of the nearly 250 pieces by Schiaparelli, more than three-quarters of them are from her wardrobe. Rogers, who was the granddaughter of Henry Huttleston Rogers, founder, along with William and John D. Rockefeller, of Standard Oil, had the means to buy fine couture clothing and the confidence and panache to wear even the most extreme examples.

Rogers originally was introduced to the Brooklyn Museum by Charles James in the mid-1940s. In 1951, after an initial gift exclusively of his works in 1949, she donated approximately sixty items, nearly all by Schiaparelli. Soon after her death three years later, her sons Arturo and Paul Peralta-Ramos made two subsequent gifts consisting of the remainder of her couture wardrobe and including more than 120 additional Schiaparelli fashions. The items in the three gifts represent all wardrobe categories—day and evening dresses and jackets, crisply tailored daytime and theater suits, and sporty sweaters. With

Opposite: Detail (front waist), Elsa Schiaparelli, *Dinner Dress*, 1940

a few notable and important exceptions, they date from 1936 to 1941. Some of the most iconic examples are an evening dress embroidered in metallic threads that form a score of musical notes, accessorized by a belt with a music box in the buckle, from her 1939 "Music" collection, and a clear plastic (Rhodoid) necklace crawling with colored-metal insects, part of her 1938 "Pagan" collection. The collection of sweaters and jackets together with a rare group of individual buttons and ornamental closures constitute a virtual textbook of these whimsical trademarks of her work. The artisan Jean Clément, who held degrees in painting and chemistry, worked exclusively for Schiaparelli and created most of her buttons, plastic jewelry, and belts.

Attesting to the often serendipitous nature of museum collecting, there are three exceptional Schiaparelli pieces that are not part of Rogers's wardrobe. A rare resort ensemble from 1932 comprising two silk half-dresses that wrap to make a whole and an evening gown from summer 1937 printed with butterflies—the Surrealist symbol for metamorphosis and death—were single Schiaparelli items included in the couture wardrobes gifted by two other donors. (Fortuitously, a matching butterfly parasol was in the Millicent Rogers gift.) A stunning blue velvet jacket embroidered with cosmic imagery associated with her 1938 "Zodiac" theme but dated summer 1937 was, on the other hand, a single gift. While museum records reveal nothing about the jacket's history aside from donor information, its impeccable condition betrays how highly valued it was to have been so carefully preserved for a period of nearly thirty-five years before it was entrusted to the Brooklyn Museum.[1]

Elsa Schiaparelli
(French, born Italy, 1890–1973)

Evening Coat, Winter 1932–33

Red silk velvet; sable; label: "Schiaparelli/4. rue de la Paix/Paris/12673"
Formerly collection of Millicent Huttleston Rogers
Brooklyn Museum Costume Collection at The Metropolitan Museum of Art, Gift of the Brooklyn Museum, 2009; Gift of Arturo and Paul Peralta-Ramos, 1954 (2009.300.1858)

Schiaparelli had an especially strong rapport with her American retail and private clients. Acknowledging their plight during Prohibition, she dubbed her winter 1932–33 collection "Speakeasy." It included designs with small squared-off back bustles that suggested a place to conceal a contraband flask. In its October 15, 1932, issue, *Vogue* referred to the color, named "cabbage red," as one of her "queer autumn shades." The coat is also an early example of Schiaparelli's emphasis on shoulder width, which became a signature silhouette of her tailored clothes throughout the 1930s. Here the sharp shoulder line is augmented by sable skins, adding both width and a luxurious aspect to the design.

Elsa Schiaparelli
(French, born Italy, 1890–1973)
By Jean Clément (French, 1900–1949)

Ornamental Fasteners in the Shape of Candlesticks, 1938

Black painted metal alloy; red glass; clear plastic cord; silver-tone metal wire
Formerly collection of Millicent Huttleston Rogers
Brooklyn Museum Costume Collection at The Metropolitan Museum of Art, Gift of the Brooklyn Museum, 2009; Gift of Arturo and Paul Peralta-Ramos, 1955 (2009.300.1501a, b)

Ornamental Fasteners in the Shape of Hand Mirrors, 1938

Black painted metal alloy; mirror glass
Formerly collection of Millicent Huttleston Rogers
Brooklyn Museum Costume Collection at The Metropolitan Museum of Art, Gift of the Brooklyn Museum, 2009; Gift of Arturo and Paul Peralta-Ramos, 1955 (2009.300.1502a, b)

These two examples of Schiaparelli's trademark ornamental fasteners could be used as alternatives on her suit jackets.

Elsa Schiaparelli
(French, born Italy, 1890–1973)

Coat, 1932–35

Cream corded cotton; gold and
copper-tone metal; label: "Schiaparelli/
4. rue de la Paix/Paris/18207"
Formerly collection of Millicent
Huttleston Rogers
Brooklyn Museum Costume Collection
at The Metropolitan Museum of Art, Gift
of the Brooklyn Museum, 2009; Gift of
Arturo and Paul Peralta-Ramos, 1955
(2009.300.1212)

Buttons and fasteners, innovative in
both design and choice of materials,
were hallmarks of Schiaparelli's
oeuvre. In perhaps one of her most
audacious decorative statements, she
recycled bullet casings to serve as
buttons and raised functional flapped
pockets to waist level, as if to
suggest the front of a hunting jacket.

Baron Adolf de Meyer (American, born France, 1868–1949).
Gloria Swanson, ca. 1934. Formerly in the collection of Sir Cecil
Beaton, Salisbury, England. Brandau, Robert, ed. *De Meyer*.
New York: Alfred A. Knopf, 1976, plate 51

Pantsuit, 1939–40

Brown and white wool tweed; brown
leather buttons; label: "Schiaparelli/
21.place vendôme/Paris/70048"
Formerly collection of Millicent
Huttleston Rogers
Brooklyn Museum Costume Collection
at The Metropolitan Museum of Art, Gift
of the Brooklyn Museum, 2009; Gift of
Arturo and Paul Peralta-Ramos, 1955
(2009.300.1870a, b)

Schiaparelli paired one of her signature structured jackets with man-
tailored cuffed pants for this only
slightly feminized version of a man's
tweed suit. Although in the 1930s
pants were accepted attire as separates for casual and sports-related
activities, pantsuits as fashion were
uncommon—only for the most
unconventional couturière and
style-confident client. While the
wearing of pants by women increasingly gained acceptance from the
1940s onward, it was not until
the 1970s that pantsuits, introduced
by couturiers Yves Saint Laurent
and André Courrèges in the mid-
1960s, became mainstream fashion.

Elsa Schiaparelli
(French, born Italy, 1890–1973),
Buttons probably by Jean Clément
(French, 1900–1949)

Sweater, 1938–40

Orange wool knit; orange ceramic buttons
Formerly collection of Millicent Huttleston Rogers
Brooklyn Museum Costume Collection at The
Metropolitan Museum of Art, Gift of the Brooklyn
Museum, 2009; Gift of Arturo and Paul
Peralta-Ramos, 1955 (2009.300.1869)

In 1927, her inaugural year, Schiaparelli
designed a sporty sweater that featured a
trompe l'oeil bow, collar, and cuffs. The success of the sweater launched her career.
Similarly, a trompe l'oeil fur collar resembling
Persian lamb is worked into this design. The
handmade ceramic buttons stamped with
"Schiap" represent her forward-thinking
approach to branding.

Sweater, 1938–40

Buttons probably by Jean Clément (French, 1900–1949)
Fuchsia wool knit, gray wool embroidery, geometric
pattern; gray ceramic buttons
Formerly collection of Millicent Huttleston Rogers
Brooklyn Museum Costume Collection at The
Metropolitan Museum of Art, Gift of the Brooklyn
Museum, 2009; Gift of Arturo and Paul Peralta-Ramos,
1954 (2009.300.1857)

Following the form of traditional Tyrolean
jackets, this sweater was custom designed for
Millicent Rogers, who lived in the Tyrolean
Alps for the second half of the 1930s. She is
known to have paired traditional dirndl skirts
or nineteenth-century Provençal petticoats
with Schiaparelli's outré tops. S-shaped buttons
announce the maker, a bold and innovative
marketing idea probably considered crass
in the 1930s.

Elsa Schiaparelli
(French, born Italy, 1890–1973)

Dress, 1939–41

Powder blue plain weave cotton;
polychrome seed packet appliqués
Brooklyn Museum Costume Collection
at The Metropolitan Museum of Art, Gift
of the Brooklyn Museum, 2009; Gift of
Millicent Huttleston Rogers, 1951
(2009.300.146)

In her 1954 autobiography, *Shocking
Life*, Schiaparelli recounts a childhood episode in which she plants
flower seeds in her mouth so that
they will grow into a garden on her
face. Evoking that early fantasy, she
cut designs from a fabric custom-
printed with flower seed packets
and applied them in scattershot
fashion on this simple summer
dress. One appliqué functions as a
pocket on the right side. A con-
spicuous gold zipper runs the full
length of the back.

Detail (back, with zipper)

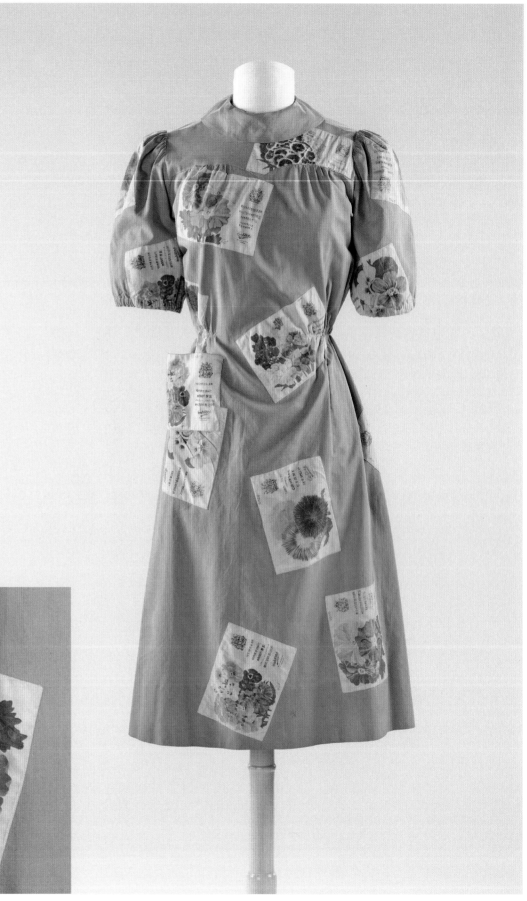

Evening Dress, Summer 1937

Ivory crepe-back silk satin printed with multicolored butterflies; label: "Schiaparelli/21.place vendôme/Paris/Été 1937"
Brooklyn Museum Costume Collection at The Metropolitan Museum of Art, Gift of the Brooklyn Museum, 2009; Gift of Mrs. Edward G. Sparrow, 1969 (2009.300.1347a, b)

Parasol, Summer 1937

Off-white cotton broadcloth printed with multicolored butterflies; wood; bamboo; label: "Schiaparelli/21.place vendôme/Paris/143962"
Formerly collection of Millicent Huttleston Rogers
Brooklyn Museum Costume Collection at The Metropolitan Museum of Art, Gift of the Brooklyn Museum, 2009; Gift of Arturo and Paul Peralta-Ramos, 1955 (2009.300.1224)

The butterfly was a ubiquitous motif in Schiaparelli's work and, for the Surrealists, a symbol of transformation and sometimes of death. Schiaparelli used it decoratively to represent beauty emerging from the mundane. It expressed her philosophy that although everyone could not be naturally beautiful, chic clothes and a sense of style could transform the ordinary into the extraordinary. At the same time, the ultrarealism of the print points up the incongruity that lifelike insects, not romanticized interpretations, are the slightly unsettling motifs on this elegant evening dress and parasol.

Music was the theme of Schiaparelli's fall 1939 collection. Correspondingly, she designed this white organza dress and gloves embroidered in metallic threads with musical-score notes and accessorized with a belt containing a working music box in the buckle. Cutout scrollwork shapes on the buckle top relate to those on a violin, forms immortalized in Man Ray's 1924 photograph "Le Violin d'Ingres." An elaboration upon the Surrealist notion of woman's body as musical instrument, the wholly integrated creation captures the visual, audible, and transcendent essence of music in the person of the wearer.

Elsa Schiaparelli
(French, born Italy, 1890–1973)

Embroidery by House of Lesage
(French, founded 1924)

Evening Dress, Fall 1939

White silk organza; polychrome metallic thread and foil embroidery; white suede; green metal housing music box; label: "Schiaparelli"
Brooklyn Museum Costume Collection at The Metropolitan Museum of Art, Gift of the Brooklyn Museum, 2009; Gift of Millicent Huttleston Rogers, 1951 (2009.300.1165a, b)

Gloves, Fall 1939

White silk organza; polychrome metallic thread and foil embroidery
Brooklyn Museum Costume Collection at The Metropolitan Museum of Art, Gift of the Brooklyn Museum, 2009; Purchase, Costume Collection Fund, 1995 (2009.300.1388a, b)

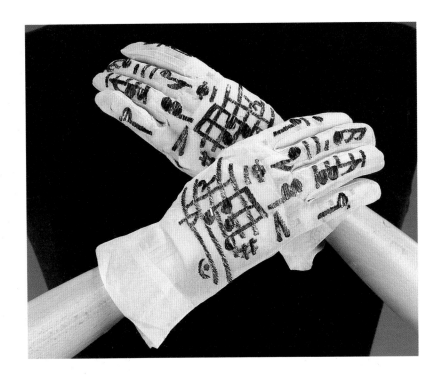

Belt (above, buckle detail side view), Fall 1939

Black suede; black metal buckle housing music box; label: "Thorens"
Formerly collection of Millicent Huttleston Rogers
Brooklyn Museum Costume Collection at The Metropolitan Museum of Art, Gift of the Brooklyn Museum, 2009; Gift of Arturo and Paul Peralta-Ramos, 1955 (2009.300.1226)

Rogers had two music-box belts in her wardrobe, one black with a black buckle (above), and one white with a green buckle (at left).

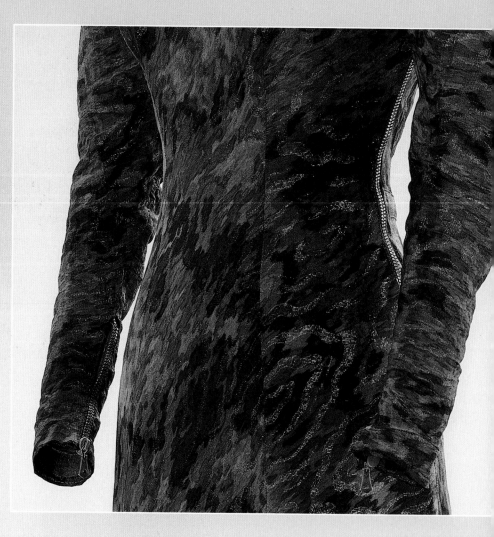

Elsa Schiaparelli
(French, born Italy, 1890–1973)

Shoes by André Perugia
(French, 1893–1977)

Dinner Ensemble, 1933–35

Green and black silk faille, supplementary gold metallic wood-grain pattern.
Shoes: green and black silk faille; gold kidskin; label: "Padova/Modele/André
Perugia/4. rue de la Paix-Paris"
Brooklyn Museum Costume Collection at The Metropolitan Museum of Art,
Gift of the Brooklyn Museum, 2009; Gift of Millicent Huttleston Rogers, 1951
(2009.300.1168a–c)

Custom textiles such as this one were important vehicles of expression for Schiaparelli. A mottled pattern of deep greens injected with
a glittering gold wood-grain motif transmogrifies the human body,
like a fleeing Daphne, into a tree. Deploying industrial zippers as
decoration on evening wear was an early iconoclastic gesture that
became a signature Schiaparelli design element.

Elsa Schiaparelli

(French, born Italy, 1890–1973)

Embroidery by House of Lesage

(French, founded 1924)

Evening Jacket, Summer 1937

Deep blue silk velvet; rhinestones; microbeads; clear plastic star-shaped paillettes, gold and silver strip embroidery; label: "Schiaparelli/21.place vendôme/Paris/Été 1937/68368"
Brooklyn Museum Costume Collection at The Metropolitan Museum of Art, Gift of the Brooklyn Museum, 2009; Gift of Mrs. Anthony V. Lynch, 1971 (2009.300.1354)

Schiaparelli developed a lifelong interest in the heavens from her uncle, Giovanni Schiaparelli, a prominent astronomer. Typically mining her childhood experiences as source material for her creative life, she used celestial iconography in several collections between 1935 and 1940. In crafting this jacket, a collaboration with master embroiderers Albert and Marie-Louise Lesage, she designed her ultimate personal and artistic expression of the theme. Surrounded by a midnight blue galaxy sprinkled with beadwork stardust, silver and gold planets, rhinestone crescent moons, swirling comets, and shooting stars, twelve glyphs representing the signs of the zodiac are embroidered in gold at center front. Ursa Major, the constellation known as the Big Dipper, which Schiaparelli adopted as her personal emblem in childhood, illuminates the left shoulder.

Detail (left back)

Illustrative of Schiaparelli's multi-layered marketing approach, these two dresses were sketched by the Surrealist artist Leonor Fini (1908–1996) and featured in a spread in "Harper's Bazaar" (see details). Fini's aesthetic is apparent in the bizarre four-legged creatures that the models tentatively constrain on pink ribbon leashes. The dresses were also marketed in connection with "Sleeping," the perfume Schiaparelli launched that same season. It was packaged in her new blue color, which she named "Sleeping Blue." The pink bolero jacket pictured on the opposite page was also available in the new color.

Elsa Schiaparelli

(French, born Italy, 1890–1973)

Dinner Dress, Summer 1940

Red matte silk jersey; aqua blue silk faille; red, white, and gold-tone ceramic buttons; blue plastic zipper; label: "Schiaparelli/21.place vendôme/Paris/Été 1940/73.6.54" Formerly collection of Millicent Huttleston Rogers Brooklyn Museum Costume Collection at The Metropolitan Museum of Art, Gift of the Brooklyn Museum, 2009; Gift of Arturo and Paul Peralta-Ramos, 1955 (2009.300.1210)

A lobster-red bodice with crustacean-like shirring combined with marine blue and fish-head motif buttons define the aquatic theme of this evening dress from Schiaparelli's summer 1940 collection. Her new slinky silhouette, called "the mermaid," featured a skirt constricted at the knees before flaring into fullness, as rendered in the Fini drawings. Although this version does not have a form-fitting skirt, the allusion to the mythological siren of the sea is clear. It also recalls the legendary white organza dress printed with a large lobster on the skirt front, which she created with Salvatore Dalí in 1937.

Leonor Fini (Italian, born Argentina, 1908–1996). Dinner dress by Elsa Schiaparelli. *Harper's Bazaar*, March 15, 1940, p. 43. Courtesy of *Harper's Bazaar*, Hearst Communications, Inc. © 2010/© 2010 Artists Rights Society (ARS), New York–ADAGP, Paris

Dinner Ensemble, Summer 1940

Jacket: pink wool twill embroidered with variably shaped black faceted beads; label: "Schiaparelli/21.place vendôme/Paris/Été 1940/73659"; Dress: black ribbed weave silk crepe; flat black plastic beads; Hat: black silk maline; faceted black plastic beads; label: "Schiaparelli/21.place vendôme/Paris/Été 1940

Brooklyn Museum Costume Collection at The Metropolitan Museum of Art, Gift of the Brooklyn Museum, 2009; Gift of Millicent Huttleston Rogers, 1951 (2009.300.1169a, b; 2009.300.1164)

Inspired by Spanish traditional dress, the cut and beadwork decoration of the jacket suggest the matador's costume, known as the "suit of lights," which was encrusted with opulent embroidery. The hat was included as part of the original concept in the house sketch of the ensemble.

Leonor Fini (Italian, born Argentina, 1908–1996). Dinner dress by Elsa Schiaparelli. *Harper's Bazaar*, March 15, 1940, p. 42. Courtesy of *Harper's Bazaar*, Hearst Communications, Inc. © 2010/© 2010 Artists Rights Society (ARS), New York–ADAGP, Paris

Elsa Schiaparelli
(French, born Italy, 1890–1973)

"Sleeping de Schiaparelli" Perfume Bottle, 1940–50

Glass, metal, paper, synthetic; label: "Perfume/Made in France"; inscription: "Schiaparelli les Parfums"
Brooklyn Museum Costume Collection at The Metropolitan Museum of Art, Gift of the Brooklyn Museum, 2009; Gift of Mrs. William R. Liberman, 1995 (2009.300.1389a–e)

Perfumes in imaginative packaging played a central role in promoting the Schiaparelli brand. She introduced "Sleeping" in the summer of 1940. Evoking in its container design a portable candleholder and cone-shaped snuffer used in the days before electricity, the perfume was a night fragrance that, according to advertisements, would illuminate the subconscious and "light the way to ecstasy." On a less literal level, the candle, as Richard Martin notes in *Fashion and Surrealism* (1987), represents the dark-to-light transition from the sleeping to the wakened mind. The candle-shaped bottles were of Baccarat crystal. Marcel Vertès produced numerous whimsical drawings for the "Sleeping" advertising campaign, one of which is illustrated below.

Marcel Vertès (French, born Hungary, 1895–1961). *Sleeping de Schiaparelli* advertisement. *Vogue*, October 15, 1946 (Advance Retail Trade Edition), p. 91. Marcel Vertès/Condé Nast Archive, © Condé Nast Publications

Evening Dress, ca. 1948

Lavender faille and white satin striped silk
Brooklyn Museum Costume Collection at The Metropolitan Museum
of Art, Gift of the Brooklyn Museum, 2009; Gift of Claire Ramsay
Roman, 1986 (2009.300.2923)

Having featured bustle dresses in her summer 1939 collection, Schiaparelli picked up where she left off before the war with this 1948 version. With fabric swept back into a low, gathered bow, it differs from the earlier designs, which featured large puffs similar to the Victorian bustles of the 1870s. An illusory X-ray image effected through placement, color, and varying surface textures of the stripes evince Schiaparelli's persisting fascination with Surrealist ideation.

These necklaces are from Schiaparelli's "Pagan" collection of 1938, which was rife with representations of flora and fauna referencing the lush imagery and mythological figures painted by Florentine artist Sandro Botticelli (1445–1510) in "The Birth of Venus" and "Primavera."

Elsa Schiaparelli
(French, born Italy, 1890–1973)
By Jean Clément (French, 1900–1949)

Necklace, Fall 1938

Clear Rhodoid (cellulose acetate plastic); metallic green, red, pink, blue, and yellow painted pressed metal ornaments
Formerly collection of Millicent Huttleston Rogers
Brooklyn Museum Costume Collection at The Metropolitan Museum of Art, Gift of the Brooklyn Museum, 2009; Gift of Arturo and Paul Peralta-Ramos, 1955
(2009.300.1234)

Rhodoid was a newly developed material that suited Schiaparelli's design intent for this necklace, perhaps her most macabre and certainly one of her most iconic designs. A transparent foundation creates the illusion that insects are crawling on the wearer's skin. Never too heavy-handed, Schiaparelli chose brightly colored toylike ornaments that temper the repugnant effect.

Necklace, Fall 1938

Gilt metal with rust and green plastic enameling
Brooklyn Museum Costume Collection at The
Metropolitan Museum of Art, Gift of the Brooklyn
Museum, 2009; Gift of Arturo and Paul
Peralta-Ramos, 1955 (2009.300.1237)

A lone cricket crawling in the foliage adds a
discomfiting touch to this otherwise elegant
design. In what may represent Schiaparelli's
influence on Surrealist artist Leonor Fini,
whose talents Schiaparelli drew upon starting in the mid-1930s, Fini's work of the
1940s portrays similar imagery, particularly
her 1942 painting *Portrait de Stanislao Lepri*.

Necklace, Fall 1938

Gilt metal with red and green plastic enameling
Brooklyn Museum Costume Collection at The
Metropolitan Museum of Art, Gift of the Brooklyn
Museum, 2009; Gift of Arturo and Paul
Peralta-Ramos, 1955 (2009.300.1236)

In pagan cultures ivy symbolized growth,
determination, and death because it could
overpower and kill larger species. The superb
workmanship of this necklace captures the
sinuous intertwining growth pattern that is
ivy's source of strength and endurance.

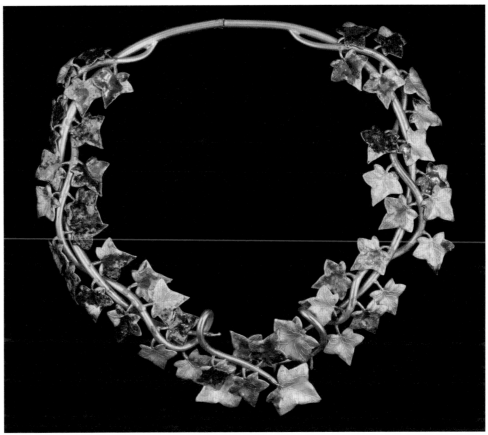

Elsa Schiaparelli
(French, born Italy, 1890–1973)
Probably by Jean Clément
(French, 1900–1949)

Evening Belt, ca. 1938

Cream calfskin painted with lavender,
pink, and black; cream calfskin lining
Brooklyn Museum Costume Collection at
The Metropolitan Museum of Art, Gift of
the Brooklyn Museum, 2009; Gift of
Arturo and Paul Peralta-Ramos, 1955
(2009.300.1228)

Unexpected displacements of
objects from their usual contexts
typified Surrealist iconography.
Here the long stem of a carnation
wraps illogically around the waist,
placing the flower in a similarly
odd position on the body. Gradual
pastel shading and childlike line
drawing are specialized artisanal
effects augmenting this fanciful
impression.

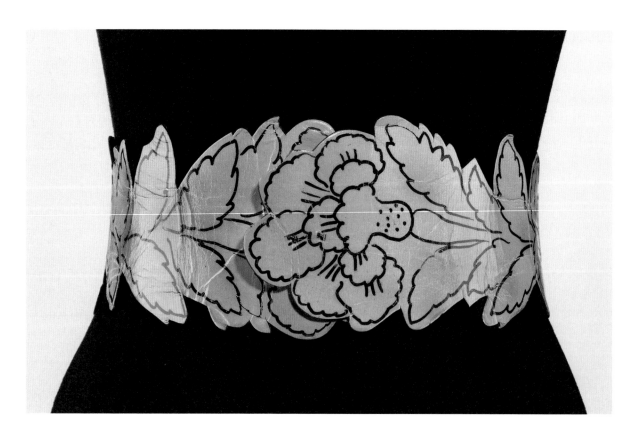

Belt, Fall 1934

Black silk double-sided taffeta, clear Lucite
Formerly collection of Millicent
Huttleston Rogers
Brooklyn Museum Costume Collection at
The Metropolitan Museum of Art, Gift of
the Brooklyn Museum, 2009; Gift of
Arturo and Paul Peralta-Ramos, 1955
(2009.300.1227)

As Richard Martin notes in *Fashion
and Surrealism* (1987), separated and
migratory body parts—particularly
eyes, lips, hands, feet—are essential
elements in the Surrealists' philosophy of transmutation. Here the
wearer is given an extra pair of perfectly manicured hands, which are
demurely folded upon each other
at the waist in a seeming state of
repose. This design has inspired
many subsequent interpretations.

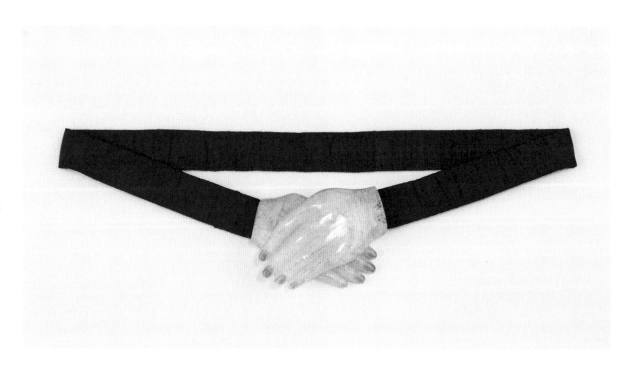

Belt, ca. 1938

Brown suede; gilt metal; plaster composition bull ornament, carved details
Brooklyn Museum Costume Collection at The Metropolitan Museum of Art, Gift of the Brooklyn Museum, 2009; Gift of Arturo and Paul Peralta-Ramos, 1955 (2009.300.1229)

A charging bull faces off against a buckle, whose curved form and pointed prong suggest the matador's cape and lance.

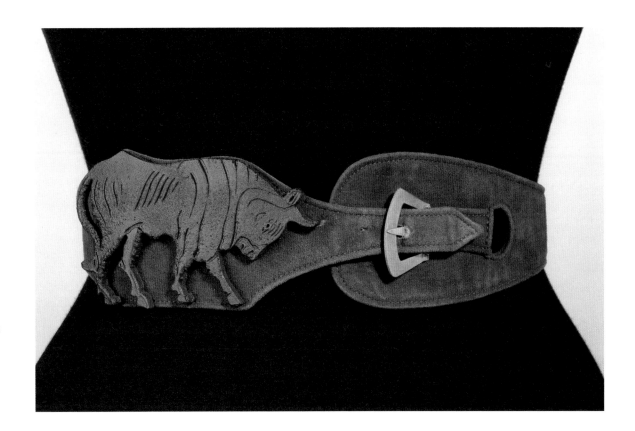

Belt, Summer 1936

Probably by Jean Clément
(French, 1900–1949)
Black plastic; cream carved plastic
Formerly collection of Millicent Huttleston Rogers
Brooklyn Museum Costume Collection at The Metropolitan Museum of Art, Gift of the Brooklyn Museum, 2009; Gift of Arturo and Paul Peralta-Ramos, 1955 (2009.300.1225)

An incongruous technique calls attention to the innovative materials used in this belt. While the color and texture of the plastic buckle imitate ivory, the rough-hewn quality of carving was a style more apt to have been worked on wood. Serpentlike rendering of the horse heads typifies Schiaparelli's inherent unconventionality.

Elsa Schiaparelli
(French, born Italy, 1890–1973)

Hat, Winter 1938–39

Black wool felt; pink, blue, white, yellow, brown, and green feathers; label: "Schiaparelli/21.place vendôme/Paris/Hiver 1938–39"
Brooklyn Museum Costume Collection at The Metropolitan Museum of Art, Gift of the Brooklyn Museum, 2009; Gift of Millicent Huttleston Rogers, 1951 (2009.300.1163)

The impression of birds dive-bombing into the crown of a Tyrolean hat epitomizes the Schiaparelli, and Rogers, wit.

Hat, Fall 1939

Black horsehair; black straw net; white and beige silk flowers; label: "Schiaparelli/21.place vendôme/Paris/Automne 1939"
Formerly collection of Millicent Huttleston Rogers
Brooklyn Museum Costume Collection at The Metropolitan Museum of Art, Gift of the Brooklyn Museum, 2009; Gift of Arturo and Paul Peralta-Ramos, 1955 (2009.300.1232)

This hat has the basic shape of the sporty sailor hat, a perennial fashion favorite since the 1880s. It was typically constructed of straw and decorated with a single ribbon wrapped around the crown. Changing the sartorial context, Schiaparelli fashioned a version from uncharacteristic horsehair and decorated it with elegant silk irises.

Hat, Fall 1939

Burgundy velvet ribbon; black, red, and
green celluloid grape clusters; artificial leaves;
label: "Schiaparelli/21.place vendôme/Paris"
Formerly collection of Millicent
Huttleston Rogers
Brooklyn Museum Costume Collection at
The Metropolitan Museum of Art, Gift of
the Brooklyn Museum, 2009; Gift of Arturo
and Paul Peralta-Ramos, 1955 (2009.300.1871)

Grape clusters are seemingly placed
spontaneously on the head, as if by
a reveler at a bacchanal.

Hat, Summer 1940

Black plaited straw; blue grosgrain ribbon;
pink, yellow, lavender, and white flowers
and buds; navy blue net veiling; label:
"Schiaparelli/21.place vendôme/Paris/Été
1940"
Brooklyn Museum Costume Collection at
The Metropolitan Museum of Art, Gift of
the Brooklyn Museum, 2009; Gift of
Millicent Huttleston Rogers, 1951
(2009.300.1446)

Doll-sized hats like this one were
fashionable in the late 1930s and
early 1940s. Perched on top rather
than fitted on the head, they were
secured with combs, pins, or veiling. Here Schiaparelli attached a
snood at back for that purpose.
Schiaparelli's love of nature, and
especially flowers, is evident in the
beautiful and naturalistic floral
adornment.

American Women Designers 1920s–1970s

These nine individuals were the most prominent of the first-generation American women designers whose careers began between the two World Wars.[1] All but two were born in the first decade of the twentieth century.[2] Three of them—Jessie Franklin Turner, Elizabeth Hawes, and Valentina Schlee—presided over custom businesses, where they created distinctive and luxurious made-to-order clothing and in some cases accessories for affluent private clients with high-style sensibilities. Also the director of her own business, Sally Victor, one of the most successful milliners of her time, produced well-crafted yet affordable hats for a broader customer base.

Turner, who began her career designing lingerie, was known for her sensual tea gowns and evening wear as well as distinctive hand-printed and woven textile patterns interpreted from non-Western cultures. Hawes designed in a more formal manner; although, known as an iconoclast, she sometimes distinguished her work with blatantly suggestive decorative accents. Formality aside, comfort, achieved through cut, fit, and fabric choice, was a high priority for her. Valentina, operating on the couture level, combined in her work a penchant for drama with a minimalist sensibility influenced in part by the unstructured two-dimensional cuts of traditional forms of dress. Victor and Turner had close early associations with the Brooklyn Museum's design services, and later the Design Lab (see Introduction), where they studied objects for inspiration from cultures as diverse as Africa, India, and Central Asia. All of these women, developing their skills and professional contacts in the 1920s, had established businesses in New York City by the beginning of the 1930s.

Hungarian-born Eta Valer Hentz, known professionally as Mme Eta, began her career in New York in 1923. She worked as head designer for exclusive ready-to-wear rather than custom firms—most notably in a long-term partnership with top-of-the-line wholesaler Maurice Rentner—but her clothes were finished with custom techniques. In contrast to the other women mentioned here, her clothing was more decorative and structured, closer to the aesthetic of the American men designing in the 1940s.

Bonnie Cashin, Carolyn Schnurer, Vera Maxwell, and Claire McCardell each worked in various design capacities during the 1930s and rose to prominence during the 1940s, when World War II interrupted the flow of materials and inspiration coming from Europe. With manpower directed toward the war effort, more opportunities for women were created in the American design business. Schnurer, Maxwell, and Cashin started their own businesses in 1946, 1947, and 1953, respectively, while in 1940, McCardell opted to stay with Townley Frocks, her original employer, when the company agreed to use her name on the label. Working within the structure of the bustling ready-to-wear garment industry centered on New York's Seventh Avenue, they honed their innovative skills in response to wartime restrictions and shortages. From the war years and throughout their careers—which for a few extended well into the 1970s—these designers took their cues from their own multifaceted lives and from those of their contemporaries, creating day and evening wear based on the versatility, practicality, and comfort of sportswear. They stripped away unnecessary decoration, utilized comfortable care-free fabrics, invented easy-to-use closures, introduced pants for streetwear, and created multipiece ensembles that with a quick change could be transformed from casual to more formal daywear, an especially functional feature for travel. Like their contemporaries in custom fashion, each was fascinated by the simplicity and graphic nature of traditional clothing forms and patterns. After the war Maxwell, Schnurer, and Cashin traveled extensively to expand their creative horizons by observing other cultures. Collectively, the work of these three, along with McCardell, originated the uniquely American sportswear aesthetic that was to become the country's most important contribution to twentieth-century fashion.[3]

Owing to the associations that most of these women had with Brooklyn's Industrial Division and the Design Lab, the museum's holdings of their works are unparalleled in scope and quality. Maxwell, Cashin, Hentz, Schnurer, and Victor each made multiple donations of their creations; their cumulative gifts, which were donated over a span of forty years starting in 1941, include many of their seminal designs and represent the full range of their creative output. Not as extensive, but nonetheless important, the McCardell collection was initiated by the designer in 1956 and augmented by others. Undoubtedly the rarest of the holdings, however, is the singular assemblage of works by Elizabeth Hawes, which is widely regarded as definitive. Starting with a 1956 gift of several pieces from the designer, the rich array was assembled through large donations by four of her primary clients, most notably Brooklyn Museum trustee Hollis K. Thayer, anthropologist Diana S. Field, and women's rights advocate Elinor S. Gimbel.

In its depth and variety, Brooklyn's collection of works by these pioneer designing women elucidates the early history of twentieth-century American fashion and makes palpable their remarkable energy, imagination, inventiveness, and independence of spirit.

Jessie Franklin Turner
(American, 1881–ca. 1956)

Evening Ensemble, ca. 1930

Black and white silk slipper satin; label: "Jessie Franklin Turner/
290 Park Avenue/NewYork"
Brooklyn Museum Costume Collection at The Metropolitan
Museum of Art, Gift of the Brooklyn Museum, 2009; Gift of the
estate of Mary Boocock Leavitt, 1974 (2009.300.511a–c)

While this luxurious slipper-satin dress epitomizes the
look and drama of 1930s evening wear, the unlikely
pairing of versatility with glamour distinguishes it. The
slinky white sleeveless garment faced with black is
accompanied by two long-sleeved overpieces, one white
with black facing and one black with white sleeves, each
of which can be worn on top of the dress bodice to
modify the silhouette, amount of skin exposure, and
proportion of black to white, thereby accommodating
the sartorial requirements of any after-hours event. The
overall Japanese aesthetic stems from Turner's early
travels in Asia.

Jessie Franklin Turner
(American, 1881–ca. 1956)

Evening Dress, ca. 1933

Gold lamé
Brooklyn Museum Costume Collection at The
Metropolitan Museum of Art, Gift of the Brooklyn
Museum, 2009; Gift of the estate of Mary Boocock
Leavitt, 1974 (2009.300.512)

Gold lamé cut on the bias drapes alluringly over
the body like liquid metal in this exemplar of
1930s style. Its sensuality is reinforced by the
slashed bolero effect of the bodice, which exposes
areas of the shoulders and arms, leaving the illusion that the wearer's arms are covered with
opera-length gloves rather than sleeves.

Elizabeth Hawes
(American, 1903–1971)

"Le Gaulois" Evening Dress, ca. 1938

Purple silk faille; label: "Hawes Incorporated"
Brooklyn Museum Costume Collection at The
Metropolitan Museum of Art, Gift of the Brooklyn
Museum, 2009; Gift of Mrs. George B. Wells, 1957
(2009.300.1935)

Hawes favored the use of integral construction
techniques rather than external decorations to
create visual interest. Here distinctive fringes
woven at the edges of silk faille stripes and lively
geometric patterns formed by skillful piecing and
mitering make up the decorative effect.

Elizabeth Hawes

(American, 1903–1971)

"The Tarts" Dress, 1937

Dark olive green silk crepe, red and purple silk satin
Brooklyn Museum Costume Collection at The
Metropolitan Museum of Art, Gift of the Brooklyn
Museum, 2009; Gift of Diana S. Field, 1964 (2009.300.872)

Known for her outspoken feminist ideas and
independent spirit, Hawes attracted like-minded
clients. Paradoxically, her design aesthetic
includes unusually suggestive motifs. The
brightly colored front and back appliquéd arrow
motifs, which draw attention to erogenous zones,
announce unabashedly the awareness of herself
as a sensual being.

Sketch for "The Tarts" dress, 1937, by Elizabeth Hawes. Watercolor and pencil. Brooklyn
Museum Libraries. Special Collections

Elizabeth Hawes
(American, 1903–1971)

"Diamond Horseshoe" Evening Dress, Fall/Winter 1936

Ivory silk crepe and chiffon, gold metallic; label: "Hawes Incorporated"
Brooklyn Museum Costume Collection at The Metropolitan Museum of Art, Gift of the Brooklyn Museum, 2009; Gift of the estate of Elinor S. Gimbel, 1984 (2009.300.1009)

"Diamond Horseshoe" is a fine example of Hawes's mastery of piecing to effect both a garment's shape and its decorative interest. Narrow bias-cut strips of silk crepe outlined with gold metallic piping curve from the front around the fitted torso to the back, where they fall in gradually widening gores to a voluminous skirt hem. The back interest serves to ensure a dramatic exit for the wearer.

Sketch for "Diamond Horseshoe" evening dress, fall/winter 1936, by Elizabeth Hawes. Watercolor, pencil, and ink. Brooklyn Museum Libraries. Special Collections

Valentina Schlee
(American, born Russia, ca. 1904–1989)

Ensemble, ca. 1942

Rose and beige wool jersey; label: "Valentina"
Brooklyn Museum Costume Collection at
The Metropolitan Museum of Art, Gift of
the Brooklyn Museum, 2009; Gift of the
estate of Mary Boocock Leavitt, 1974
(2009.300.510a–c)

Characteristic of the inherent sensuality of Valentina's work, the soft drape of jersey, rounded shoulders, and muted earth tones of this suit deftly mitigate the rigorous masculine lines and economical use of materials characteristic of the war years. She reserved the rigor for the sharp geometry of the jacket construction, in which the sleeves and angular piecing are cut in one. A signature headwear design, the soft thimble-shaped matching hat resembling a turban, provides an additional touch of allure.

Evening Dress, ca. 1935

Ivory silk jersey; label: "Valentina"
Formerly collection of Millicent
Huttleston Rogers
Brooklyn Museum Costume Collection at
The Metropolitan Museum of Art, Gift of
the Brooklyn Museum, 2009; Gift of
Arturo and Paul Peralta-Ramos, 1954
(2009.300.190)

The timeless quality of Valentina's work is here reiterated in her interpretation of classical dress.

As if the designer had draped them standing in front of a Greek or Roman sculpture, the curved folds fall in imitation of their counterparts chiseled in marble. The bodice, fitted with seams and darts, appears deceptively to be bound to the torso by crisscrossing bands, alluding to the long wrap ties in antique dress that served that function.

In keeping with the design community's heightened interest in American museum resources during World War II, Mme Eta created both of these dresses in conjunction with an architectural exhibition entitled "The Greek Revival in the United States," held at The Metropolitan Museum of Art from November 1943 to March 1944. Mannequins in period clothing were part of the installation. According to a press release (now in the Brooklyn Museum Archives) written by fashion publicist Eleanor Lambert, the designer was given access to the source material used to plan the exhibition. Both of these gowns were photographed for "Vogue" in the Metropolitan's galleries.

Cocktail dress by Madame Eta Hentz, 1944. The Brooklyn Museum Libraries. Artist Files

Madame Eta Hentz

(American, born Hungary) for Ren-Eta Gowns, Inc.

Dress, Spring/Summer 1944

Navy and white rayon
Brooklyn Museum Costume Collection at The Metropolitan Museum of Art, Gift of the Brooklyn Museum, 2009; Gift of Madame Eta Hentz, 1946 (2009.300.118a, b)

The interlocking wing design rendered in striking contrast down the full length of this late-day dress is interpreted from a period costume shown in the 1943–44 Greek Revival exhibition at the Metropolitan Museum. Although the specific nineteenth-century dress is not known, the design is consistent with the type rendered in the horizontal hem sculpture of dresses from the mid- to late 1820s. This vertical interpretation enlivens the regulated minimalism of the wartime silhouette.

Evening Dress, Spring/Summer 1944

Cream rayon crepe; gold-colored beads, laurel leaf pattern
Brooklyn Museum Costume Collection at The Metropolitan Museum of Art, Gift of the Brooklyn Museum, 2009; Gift of Madame Eta Hentz, 1946 (2009.300.119)

This elegant evening dress adapts the classical aesthetic to a modern sensibility. Incorporating elements of the Greek chiton (tunic) and himation (cloak), the dress's body-hugging form and elaborate bead-work update it to the prevailing look for important evenings. In the same press release (mentioned on the previous page), Eleanor Lambert wrote: "One dress of white sheer wraps the figure closely, leaving one shoulder bare while a long scarf hangs from the other. A deep band of gold beading points up the fact that the dress has two hemlines, one slanting from the calf to the knee, the other a pleated flounce touching the floor."

John Rawlings (American, 1912–1970). Evening dresses by Madame Eta Hentz. *Vogue*, February 1, 1944, p. 68. John Rawlings/Condé Nast Archive, © Condé Nast Publications

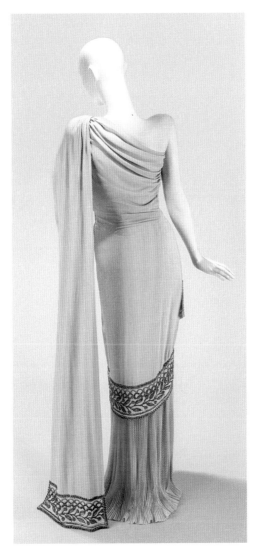

Claire McCardell

(American, 1905–1958)

Pants Ensemble, 1941

Beige wool twill
Brooklyn Museum Costume Collection at The
Metropolitan Museum of Art, Gift of the Brooklyn
Museum, 2009; Gift of Claire McCardell, 1956
(2009.300.229a, b)

While pants were worn as separates for casual
and sports-related activities in the 1920s and
1930s, McCardell brought them into the fashion
arena with this ensemble that creates a total look.
While it has a casual air, the open welt seaming
on the sleeves and the closed jewel neck are
dressy touches. More convenient and stylish than
the one-piece jumpsuits that were donned by
women a year or two later for work in factories
during the war, the ensemble is an early exemplar
of McCardell's interest in easy, comfortable
clothes with panache. McCardell was largely
responsible for making pants a staple of the
American woman's wardrobe.

Ensemble, 1946

Striated oatmeal and brown wool jersey, brown cotton poplin; label: "claire mc cardell clothes/by townley" Brooklyn Museum Costume Collection at The Metropolitan Museum of Art, Gift of the Brooklyn Museum, 2009; Gift of Claire McCardell, 1956 (2009.300.231a–c)

Her name most closely associated with the "American Look," McCardell is the best known and widely considered the most influential of her generation of American women designers. As with her contemporaries, versatility, comfort, and style directed her creative philosophy. This chic ensemble of comfortable wool jersey epitomizes the fresh, modern, unpretentious approach to dressing that won her the adulation of the press and American working women and housewives in the 1940s and 1950s. Enlivened by variations in pattern rather than extraneous decorations, these versatile coordinated separates are enhanced by a reversible coat and two integral hoods, one for the coat, the other for the blouse. The latter drapes into a collar when not needed for protection from the elements.

Claire McCardell

(American, 1905–1958)

Beach Ensemble, 1944

Printed cotton
Brooklyn Museum Costume Collection at The
Metropolitan Museum of Art, Gift of the Brooklyn
Museum, 2009; Gift of Claire McCardell, 1956
(2009.300.1245a–c)

Playfulness informs the textile and function of
this example of what McCardell called her
"playclothes."

Typical of her body-conscious aesthetic, nei-
ther the dress nor the bathing suit is fitted with
any supporting understructure to cause discomfort or restrict movement. The buttons that serve
as closures on the left side of the wrap dress
whimsically repeat in three dimensions the textile's trompe l'oeil pattern of yellow buttons with
black half-rims that suggest "happy face" smiles.

Bonnie Cashin

(American, 1908–2000) with Eunice Cashin
(American)

"The Tweed Toga" Ensemble, 1943

Red, black, and white wool houndstooth plaid;
label: "Bonnie Cashin Original"
Brooklyn Museum Costume Collection at The
Metropolitan Museum of Art, Gift of the
Brooklyn Museum, 2009; Gift of Bonnie
Cashin, 1963 (2009.300.2031a–c)

Here Cashin transformed the cut of a
traditional South American poncho
into fashionable outerwear by adding a
shirt collar, front button placket, and a
pair of smart spats. Working well with
both leggings or a sleek black dress, it
adapts for sporty or late-day wear.
Adding to its versatility, Cashin
designed a matching tweed lap robe to
maintain the integrity of the ensemble
look even when extra warmth was
required. Eunice Cashin, her mother,
was an accomplished seamstress who
constructed some of Bonnie Cashin's
earlier designs.

"The Tweed Toga" ensemble by Bonnie Cashin, 1943.
Brooklyn Museum Costume Collection at The
Metropolitan Museum of Art, Courtesy of the Irene
Lewisohn Costume Reference Library

Cocktail Dress, 1953

Aqua kidskin
Brooklyn Museum Costume Collection at
The Metropolitan Museum of Art, Gift of
the Brooklyn Museum, 2009; Gift of
Bonnie Cashin, 1953 (2009.300.1256a, b)

While this handsome cocktail dress
follows the fashionable bouffant
silhouette of its time, the choice of
materials is anything but conventional. Lightweight taffetas, organ-
zas, tulles, or fine cottons were the
prevailing choices for cocktail
attire, whereas leather, because of its
durability, expense, and the special
technical skills needed to manipu-
late it, was most often utilized for
outer- and sporting wear or accessories, especially gloves. Fascinated
with its possibilities for fashion
design, Cashin began a collaboration with leather importer Philip
Sills in 1953. The dress is from her
first Sills collection, which, consisting entirely of kidskin garments,
was meant to promote the material's luxurious qualities and
adaptability for fashionable attire—
even for elegant occasions such as a
cocktail party. Constructed in two
parts, bodice and skirt, the design
features Cashin's signature cantilevered hip yoke, which she used
with all materials, to enhance the
buoyancy and fullness of her circular skirts. Even though kidskin is the
most supple of leathers, the cutting
and sewing needed to achieve the
glovelike fit of the bodice and the
symmetrical expanse of the circular
skirt are a tour de force of design
and technical expertise.

In 1946 Carolyn Schnurer inaugurated a schedule of international travels on which she based what she dubbed her "Flight" collections for resort wear. Between then and 1955 she traveled to eight destinations that included Peru, India, Japan, Ghana, and South Africa. She interpreted her observations of traditional costumes in the textiles, decoration, and construction details of her designs.

Carolyn Schnurer
(American, 1908–1998)

Sundress, 1950

Red plain weave cotton, yellow foliate borders; purple voile
Brooklyn Museum Costume Collection at The Metropolitan Museum of Art,
Gift of the Brooklyn Museum, 2009; Gift of Carolyn Schnurer, 1951
(2009.300.145)

Bathing Suit, 1950

Purple plain weave cotton, red foliate borders
Brooklyn Museum Costume Collection at The Metropolitan Museum of Art,
Gift of the Brooklyn Museum, 2009; Gift of Carolyn Schnurer, 1951
(2009.300.1162)

From Schnurer's "Flight to India" collection, this dress and matching bathing suit illustrate the designer's ability to convey the cultural theme through textile and drape. The print and colors of the textile, manufactured by ABC fabrics, are based upon a cotton voile sari that Schnurer purchased in the northern city of Ahmadabad, the largest textile-producing center in India. She expressed in her design the regional and cultural variations of draping the sari by adding the two-part sash, which can be used in several ways. Similarly, without modifying the basic bathing-suit pattern, she alludes to the sari in the convertible shoulder strap and slight hip ruffle.

Clifford Coffin (American, 1913–1972). Sundress by Carolyn Schnurer. *Glamour*, January 1951, p. 89 (detail). Clifford Coffin/Condé Nast Archive, © Condé Nast Publications

Dress, 1952

Beige sateen, interlace pattern; orange faille
Brooklyn Museum Costume Collection at The
Metropolitan Museum of Art, Gift of the Brooklyn
Museum, 2009; Gift of Carolyn Schnurer, 1952
(2009.300.1846a, b)

The crossover bodice, tubular sleeves, and wide
sash with hip-length pendants at back recall the
Japanese kimono and obi.

Beach Ensemble, 1952

Beige cotton broadcloth; beige sateen, interlace pattern
Brooklyn Museum Costume Collection at The
Metropolitan Museum of Art, Gift of the Brooklyn
Museum, 2009; Gift of Carolyn Schnurer, 1952
(2009.300.161a, b)

In the jacket of the beach ensemble from the
"Flight to Japan" collection, Schnurer referenced
the cut of those worn by students at Gakushüin,
or Peer's School, which was founded in Tokyo in
1877 originally to educate imperial and aristocratic children and later opened to commoners.
The pattern of the embroidered textile by
Hollander, used in the jacket as well as the dress,
interprets that of the plaited rice-straw raincoats
worn by rural workers and the webbing of rope
nets that secured thatched roofs. The bathing-suit
textile was inspired by the pattern on the lid of a
box containing ceremonial tea napkins.

Vera Maxwell
(American, 1901–1995)

Ensemble, ca. 1958

Black and white wool jersey; charcoal gray brushed wool; label: "Vera Maxwell Original"
Brooklyn Museum Costume Collection at The Metropolitan Museum of Art, Gift of the Brooklyn Museum, 2009; Gift of Vera Maxwell, 1959 (2009.300.270a–d)

At the heart of her philosophy that "clothes should be beautiful, adaptable and sound," Maxwell began designing what she referred to as her "travel suit" in the late 1930s and continued doing so until the end of her career. Comprising four matching and coordinating pieces, this example is a signature representation of her skill in combining style and function. Choosing comfortable and wrinkle-resistant jersey for the design, Maxwell intended pants to be worn under the skirt or alone for plane or train. Nonetheless stylish for its functionality, the wrap blouse, which she asserted was her innovation, retains a chic fit regardless of the travails of travel, and the brushed-wool overcoat is self-lined with the jersey for a completely coordinated look.

Tennis Ensemble, ca. 1976 (opposite)

Navy blue Helanca jersey; ivory Ultrasuede; label: "Vera Maxwell Original"
Brooklyn Museum Costume Collection at The Metropolitan Museum of Art, Gift of the Brooklyn Museum, 2009; Gift of Vera Maxwell, 1979 (2009.300.531a–c)

Maxwell was a sportswoman and designed sports clothing throughout her career. The dress in this ensemble is constructed from a jersey leotard and a washable Ultrasuede skirt, the simplest of garments to put on and to care for. Combined with a fashionable matching jacket, the ensemble moves with style from the court to the clubhouse for postgame socializing. Maxwell was a pioneer, along with Bonnie Cashin, in the use of Ultrasuede, which Maxwell introduced into her collections in the 1940s. The fabric did not gain wide acceptance, however, until the American designer Halston adopted it some twenty years later.

Sally Victor
(American, 1905–1977)

Hat, 1936

Red fur felt; green rayon jersey; label: "Sally Victor/18 East 53rd St."
Brooklyn Museum Costume Collection at The Metropolitan Museum
of Art, Gift of the Brooklyn Museum, 2009; Gift of Sally Victor, Inc.,
1944 (2009.300.1117)

In a seemingly spontaneous twist and thrust of apple green
jersey through red felt, Victor transformed a simple broad-
brimmed picture hat into a sophisticated sculptural form
with three distinct views. The wide brim dominates the
right side; the left side brim is turned up to the crown like a
military bicorne; and the back of the head is wrapped in
green jersey in the manner of a turban (right, top and bottom).

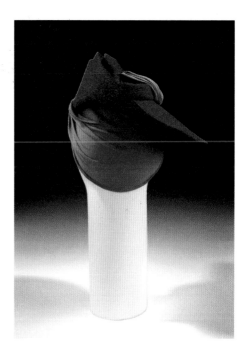

Sally Victor
(American, 1905–1977)

Hat, 1937

Navy blue straw, white piqué cotton; label: "Sally Victor/18 East 53rd St."
Brooklyn Museum Costume Collection at The Metropolitan Museum of Art, Gift of the Brooklyn Museum, 2009; Gift of Sally Victor, Inc., 1944 (2009.307.1119)

Designed in 1937, when Surrealism was at its peak, this hat was conceived by Victor in imitation of an elaborate braided hairstyle inspired by one of the many world cultures she referred to throughout her career. To establish it as fashion rather than a too literal interpretation, she chose navy blue straw and white piqué, traditionally stylish colors and materials for spring hats.

"Airwave" Hat, 1952

White and magenta wool felt; label: "Sally Victor/18 East 53rd St."
Brooklyn Museum Costume Collection at The Metropolitan Museum of Art, Gift of the Brooklyn Museum, 2009; Gift of Sally Victor, 1953 (2009.300.1175)

Victor created this design for Mrs. Dwight D. Eisenhower to wear to an American Heart Association luncheon in 1952. She subsequently wore a different version, gray with green lining, on the occasion of her husband's presidential inauguration in 1953. Along with the collapsible straw hat (opposite), it is one of several inspired by the construction of Japanese samurai armor. In a conflation of cultures and time periods, its pierced undulating form and the title Victor assigned it allude as well to industrial and architectural forms of the early 1950s.

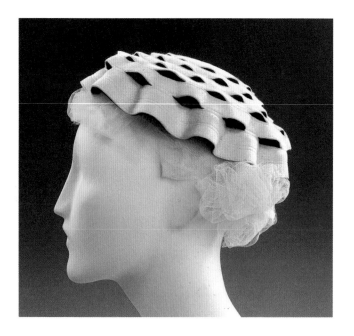

George Skadding (American, 1905–1976). Mrs. Dwight D. Eisenhower, wearing "Airwave" hat by Sally Victor, with Harry S. Truman, 1953. Time & Life Pictures/Getty Images

Hat, ca. 1945

Natural straw, black silk grosgrain; label: "Sally Victor/18 East 53rd St."
Brooklyn Museum Costume Collection at The Metropolitan Museum of Art, Gift of the Brooklyn Museum, 2009; Gift of Sally Victor, 1950 (2009.300.1161)

Intrigued by the concentric collapsible construction of some types of Japanese samurai armor, Victor created a number of hats based on its design. Like other women designers of her period, convenience and adaptability were important aspects of her process. The crown of this hat collapses, making it easy to pack flat in a suitcase for travel and equally easy to pop back into shape to be worn.

"Matisse" Hat, ca. 1962

White woven straw; royal blue wool felt appliqués; label: "Sally Victor/New York"
Brooklyn Museum Costume Collection at The Metropolitan Museum of Art, Gift of the Brooklyn Museum, 2009; Gift of the artist, 1964 (2009.300.1321)

The large upturned brim of this hat provides an ideal canvas for Victor's interpretation of the artist Henri Matisse's paper "cutouts," a technique that absorbed him late in his career.

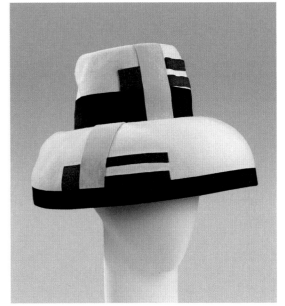

"Mondrian" Hat, ca. 1962

White fur felt; yellow, blue, and orange wool felt, black silk grosgrain ribbon; label: "Sally Victor/New York"
Brooklyn Museum Costume Collection at The Metropolitan Museum of Art, Gift of the Brooklyn Museum, 2009; Gift of the artist, 1964 (2009.300.1320)

Victor's wide repertoire of design sources included works of fine art. This hat was inspired by Piet Mondrian's grid-based paintings rendered in primary colors on a white ground. Predating Yves Saint Laurent's highly acclaimed Mondrian-inspired chemise dress of 1965, the hat is evidence that Victor still maintained a forward-thinking mentality after nearly thirty years of work. The hat's mushroom silhouette was a prevailing style that counterbalanced the simple sheath dresses of the early 1960s.

American Men Designers 1930s–1980s

The Brooklyn collection includes the work of mid-twentieth-century American men designers that corresponds in quality if not in quantity with the holdings of costumes and accessories by the American women. The group of seven men represents two generations: the first with Mainbocher (Main Rousseau Bocher), Norman Norell, and Gilbert Adrian, who had birth dates early in the century that correspond roughly to those of Jessie Franklin Turner, Elizabeth Hawes, and Valentina. Mainbocher and Adrian were well established in the 1930s—Mainbocher as a couturier in Paris and Adrian as a prominent Hollywood costume designer. In New York City during the 1930s, Norell designed for Hattie Carnegie. All three men made significant changes in their careers in the early 1940s, at the same time that women designers were beginning to exert their influence. Mainbocher moved his enterprise from Paris to New York City; Adrian established a custom and ready-to-wear fashion business in Hollywood; and Norell partnered with Anthony Traina, an exclusive ready-to-wear manufacturer in New York's Seventh Avenue garment district, to design under the label Traina-Norell.

Adrian ceased designing in 1952, but Mainbocher's and Norell's careers extended into the early 1970s, making them professional contemporaries of the next generation represented by James Galanos, Geoffrey Beene, Arnold Scaasi, and Halston (Roy Halston Frowick). Born between 1925 and 1932, they established their careers in the 1950s and early 1960s. Both generations, with the exception of Mainbocher, who worked as a couturier, designed for the high-end ready-to-wear market. Halston, Scaasi, and Adrian offered custom lines as well.

The men's designs represent postwar high-style American fashion produced at a time when French couture was once again dominant, and women, while by no means abandoning the sportswear aesthetic, were drawn to more decorative, structured, and expensive fashions appropriate for their expanding roles in the social, corporate, and entertainment worlds. They are clothes with an important presence

that put forth a polished, formal look for day and a glamorous aura worthy of grand entrances and the photographer's flash at night.

Mainbocher's work is characterized by its discreet expressions of luxury, meant to be recognized only by discerning fashion connoisseurs, while Adrian's clothes are marked by their fine cut, whimsy, and artistic manipulation of fabrics. Pared down and timeless, Norell's garments, consistently inspired by a few favorite sources, such as the sailor suit and styles of the 1920s, contrast with Galanos's more elaborate designs, culled from a widely varied repertoire of references, including traditional costume and both ancient and modern art. Yet because both men maintained personal control over their enterprises, the quality of workmanship, materials, and perfection of construction represent the pinnacle of ready-to-wear production. Halston captured the moment in the 1970s with a sportswear-inspired aesthetic for day and evening, as well as sensual, minimally cut draped evening dresses. At the other end of the spectrum, the ebullient spirit of Scaasi's unabashedly decorative and colorful aesthetic captured the imaginations of scores of celebrities and the socially prominent over five decades. Beene, probably the most avant-garde of American designers, is heralded for his dauntless inventiveness, motivated by his affinity for twentieth-century art and the desire to express it on his own terms.

Separating American designers by gender inevitably leads to considerations as to its influence upon their stylistic preferences. Despite overlaps in dates and career paths, some contrasts between the men's and women's aesthetics stand out. Whether or not these differences can be partially attributed to the designers' genders or are simply the results of social and political forces at play in the 1930s, 1940s, and 1950s is a matter worthy of consideration but beyond the scope of this essay.

As a whole the men's output represents a different point of view about dressing. Luxurious fabrics, couture-quality workmanship, and fashion-forward style take precedence over comfort, adaptability, and functionality, the primary concerns of the majority of the women. Furthermore, while most of the women designers found inspiration in the minimal two-dimensional cuts and lively patterns of traditional non-Western cultures, inspiration from American and Western European fine arts was more common in the men's work. Exceptions are Mainbocher's dresses made from the Indian sari, which became a signature design of his during the 1950s. Arguably a corollary, five of the men had formal training or significant professional experience in France, while only three of the nine women, Turner, Hawes, and McCardell, had early training in Paris. Several of the women sought inspiration in traditional cultures, and Turner, early in her career, traveled extensively in Asia.

The Brooklyn Museum's history of acquiring the men's clothing was also markedly different. As discussed in the previous chapter, several of the women designers had direct relationships with the Brooklyn Museum's Design Lab and, influenced by its leadership in the fashion field, made large donations of their work. On the other hand, the men did not associate with the Lab and, with the exception of a 1996 gift from Arnold Scaasi, did not donate directly to the collection.

Clothes by these designers were donated between 1954 and the late 1990s and for the most part came in small groups of five or fewer from individual donors. Several significant gifts are notable exceptions. Two gifts from Millicent Rogers's sons, Arturo and Paul Peralta-Ramos, included some fifty items by Mainbocher from the 1940s. These were the first from the men designers' group to enter the collection. The important Adrian pieces were given by his wife, the actress Janet Gaynor, upon a request by the curatorial consultant, Robert Riley, who was actively seeking examples of the designer's works. In a 1962 letter to Gaynor, citing "a great dearth of Adrians," he inquired whether she knew how he could obtain some for the collection. Gaynor responded by sending seven important pieces, explaining that four of the seven were made especially for her and that [she was] "sure that Adrian would be pleased to have them at the Brooklyn Museum."[1]

The actress Lauren Bacall's donations of nearly seventy-five Norells dating from 1949 to 1965 constitutes the most extensive assemblage of works by the designers in this group. Mostly from the 1950s, when both Norell and Bacall were at the heights of their careers, the many cocktail and evening examples confirm Bacall's well-proportioned slim figure as the perfect showcase for the simply cut, body-cleaving bodices of Norell's classic crinoline-skirted cocktail dresses.

Finally, Austine Hearst (Mrs. William Randolph Hearst, Jr.), social luminary, fashion leader, and philanthropist, is responsible for most of the important later works by Arnold Scaasi. A Scaasi client in the early 1980s, she contributed a dozen examples of his show-stopping cocktail and evening fashions dating from 1979 to 1984.

Mainbocher

(American, 1891–1976)

Evening Ensemble, 1949

Pink silk faille; white silk organdy; black figured silk satin;
cream and black tassel and braid passementerie; label:
"Mainbocher, Inc."
Formerly collection of Millicent Huttleston Rogers
Brooklyn Museum Costume Collection at The Metropolitan
Museum of Art, Gift of the Brooklyn Museum, 2009; Gift of
Arturo and Paul Peralta-Ramos, 1954 (2009.300.788a, b)

Millicent Rogers, the consummate woman of style,
commissioned this ensemble, an interpretation of
1830s fashion, and several other similar examples to
complement the Biedermeier period (1815–48) furni-
ture that decorated her Virginia home, "Claremont
Manor." Mainbocher's version of the X-shaped silhouette, formed by large puffed gigot sleeves, slop-
ing shoulders, and wide ankle-length skirts, is
remarkably close to the originals, with modifica-
tions in the length of the sleeves and the width
of the collar. The inclusion of tassels and swags,
found on upholstery and curtains rather than on
garments of the period, is an over-the-top touch
that may explain the text in the July 1949 issue of
Harper's Bazaar describing such ensembles as
"ornate upholstered dresses."

Louise Dahl-Wolfe (American, 1895–1989). Untitled
[Millicent Rogers] n.d. *Harper's Bazaar*, July 1949, p. 52
(variant published). Collection Center for Creative
Photography, University of Arizona. © 1989 Arizona Board
of Regents

Mainbocher
(American, 1891–1976)

Dinner Ensemble, ca. 1953

Oatmeal wool knit; brown, ivory, and blue wool tweed; muskrat fur; label: "Mainbocher, Inc." Brooklyn Museum Costume Collection at The Metropolitan Museum of Art, Gift of the Brooklyn Museum, 2009; Gift of Mrs. T. Suffern Tailer, 1967 (2009.300.29a–c)

The surprise of sparkling rhinestones and soft fur are the hidden luxuries of this dinner ensemble, revealed when the handsome, yet sober, four-button hip-length tailored jacket is removed.

Evening Belt, ca. 1943

Navy blue silk broadcloth; silk violets
Formerly collection of Millicent Huttleston Rogers
Brooklyn Museum Costume Collection at The Metropolitan Museum of Art, Gift of the
Brooklyn Museum, 2009; Gift of Arturo and Paul Peralta-Ramos, 1954 (2009.300.1868)

Evening Belt, 1944

Black silk crepe; black guipure lace; silk pink and white blossoms
Formerly collection of Millicent Huttleston Rogers
Brooklyn Museum Costume Collection at The Metropolitan Museum of Art, Gift of the
Brooklyn Museum, 2009; Gift of Arturo and Paul Peralta-Ramos, 1954 (2009.300.1867)

Evening Belt, 1943

Black wool crepe; silk white roses; label: "Mainbocher, Inc."
Formerly collection of Millicent Huttleston Rogers
Brooklyn Museum Costume Collection at The Metropolitan Museum of Art, Gift of the
Brooklyn Museum, 2009; Gift of Arturo and Paul Peralta-Ramos, 1954 (2009.300.1866)

Less than an apron but more than a belt, these examples of fantasy waist
decoration, known as "glamour belts," were used to enliven the somber
mood of wartime fashions.

Gilbert Adrian
(American, 1903–1959)

Dinner Dress, ca. 1944

Pieced pink, purple, red, gray, and brown silk pongée
Brooklyn Museum Costume Collection at The Metropolitan
Museum of Art, Gift of the Brooklyn Museum, 2009; Gift of Janet
Gaynor Adrian, 1963 (2009.300.320)

Dinner Dress, ca. 1944

Pieced gray, pink, brown, and green silk pongée; label; "Adrian
Custom"
Brooklyn Museum Costume Collection at The Metropolitan
Museum of Art, Gift of the Brooklyn Museum, 2009; Gift of Janet
Gaynor Adrian, 1963 (2009.300.319)

In 1944 Adrian created a line of dresses that was inspired
by the Cubist paintings of artists Georges Braque (1882–
1963) and Pablo Picasso (1881–1973). An artist himself,
Adrian arranged abstract shapes of fabric in juxtaposi-
tions of color and line as deftly as if they were painted
with a brush. According to Adrian's wife, the actress
Janet Gaynor (1906–1984), he made these two dresses
exclusively for her.

"The Tigress" Evening Ensemble, 1949

Black, beige, and orange silk taffeta chiné; gold lamé
Brooklyn Museum Costume Collection at The Metropolitan
Museum of Art, Gift of the Brooklyn Museum, 2009; Gift of Janet
Gaynor Adrian, 1963 (2009.300.1297a, b)

Since leopard spots, but not tiger stripes, were an occa-
sional pattern found in the sumptuous textiles that
made up the grand pannier dresses of the eighteenth
century, Adrian used poetic license in this modern rein-
terpretation of the historic silhouette. Returning to the
form that he originally worked with in his designs for
the 1938 film *Marie Antoinette*, he sculpted the skirt
panniers by employing the stiffness of the fabric rather
than the bulky understructure of the antique and film
examples. Although this ensemble was part of his 1949
fall collection, based on inspiration from his trip to
Africa earlier in the year, he famously joked that the
gown was an exception, as there are no tigers in Africa.

Clifford Coffin (American, 1913–1972). Evening ensemble by Gilbert Adrian. *Vogue*, September 15, 1949, p. 131. Clifford Coffin/Condé Nast Archive, © Condé Nast Publications

John Engstead (American, 1912–1984). Adrian advertisement. Detail. *Vogue*, September 1, 1949, p. 34. John Engstead/Condé Nast Archive, © Condé Nast Publications

Norman Norell
(American, 1900–1972)

Dinner Dress, 1951

Black wool jersey; white cotton organdy
Brooklyn Museum Costume Collection at The Metropolitan Museum of Art,
Gift of the Brooklyn Museum, 2009; Gift of Lauren Bacall, 1959
(2009.300.265)

Norell often used the crisp clean appearance of white organdy to
impart a sense of simplicity and purity to his designs. Here, he
set it in bold contrast to the sensual cling of black jersey. The
inherent tension between the buttoned-up, collared, and cuffed
primness of the bodice with the romance of the extravagant bouffant skirt and red rose is the essence of 1950s sophistication.

Evening Dress, ca. 1958

Black nylon tulle; black fox fur; label: "Nan Duskin"
Brooklyn Museum Costume Collection at The Metropolitan Museum of Art,
Gift of the Brooklyn Museum, 2009; Gift of Frances Carpenter, 1965
(2009.300.382)

In quality and luxury as well as in price, Norell was Dior's
American counterpart in the 1950s. Sparing no expense, Norell
made liberal use of fur, the ultimate luxury material, for day and
evening wear. Elaborating upon the more typical application of
fur at a garment's hem, he decorated the skirt's entirety with
incremental bands of gleaming black fox. The mathematical
precision with which the fur is applied gives the impression of
simplicity that is a hallmark of his work. Nan Duskin was an
ultra-exclusive dress shop, located on Rittenhouse Square,
Philadelphia, that carried Norell's designs.

Evening Ensemble, 1970–71

Gold organdy; beaded gold silk jersey
Brooklyn Museum Costume Collection at The Metropolitan Museum of Art,
Gift of the Brooklyn Museum, 2009; Gift of Toni Tavan Ausnit, 1990
(2009.300.1383a, b)

Two of Norell's signature fabrics, crisp organdy and glittering
silk jersey, generate the magic of this ensemble. The exaggerated
volume of sleeves and bow stand out as sculpted artistry in contrast to the fluidity and sparkle of the beaded wide-legged pants.
Designed for one of his last collections, it is testimony to Norell's
capacity for developing new forms from fabrics he favored during
his long career. As a new idea in the early 1970s, the emphatic
legitimization of pants for formal evening attire inherent in this
ensemble is likewise evidence of Norell's modernity.

James Galanos

(American, born 1925)

Evening Dress, ca. 1955

Red and white striped silk crepe and chiffon; label: "Galanos"
Brooklyn Museum Costume Collection at The Metropolitan Museum of Art, Gift of the Brooklyn Museum, 2009; Gift of Mrs. Mortimer J. Solomon, 1978 (2009.300.527)

Red and white stripes undulating like rolling waves and a jaunty knot displaced from a sailor's middy collar to the lower hem of this evening gown interpret a classic nautical theme in layers of gossamer chiffon.

Evening Dress, 1959–61

Red, pink, and marigold color-blocked silk chiffon
Brooklyn Museum Costume Collection at The Metropolitan Museum of Art, Gift of the Brooklyn Museum, 2009; Gift of Mildred Morton, 1961 (2009.300.2010)

In this allusion to contemporary artists of the 1950s and 1960s such as Josef Albers (1888–1976), who worked with geometric shapes of solid color as a design precept, Galanos was at the forefront of the 1960s fashion trend to incorporate into dress design elements taken from the fine arts.

Arnold Scaasi
(American, born Canada, 1931)

Evening Ensemble, 1961

Cream silk satin printed with red and black polka dots; red barathea; label: "Scaasi" Brooklyn Museum Costume Collection at The Metropolitan Museum of Art, Gift of the Brooklyn Museum, 2009; Gift of Kay Kerr, 1965 (2009.300.391a, b)

Scaasi's exuberant evening ensembles with bouffant dresses and self-lined swing coats are some of his most admired works. This example with polka dots akin to balloons captures the youthful spirit that was to characterize the 1960s.

Evening Ensemble, Spring/Summer 1983

Brown and pink silk taffeta; pink silk organza poppies; label: "Arnold Scaasi" Brooklyn Museum Costume Collection at The Metropolitan Museum of Art, Gift of the Brooklyn Museum, 2009; Gift of Mrs. William Randolph Hearst, Jr., 1991 (2009.300.1063a, b)

Nineteen-eighties opulence reaches its zenith in the profusion of poppies, arguably the most opulent of flowers, expertly rendered in silk organza and lavishly applied to the taffeta skirt and cape of this ensemble. Worn by the eminently fashionable philanthropist and one-time columnist Austine Hearst, the ensemble's presence would have enlivened the ambience of any occasion.

Halston
(American, 1932–1990)

Evening Dress, ca. 1975

Silk chiffon tie-dyed in orange to yellow ombré grid pattern with green diagonal stripe
Brooklyn Museum Costume Collection at The Metropolitan Museum of Art, Gift of the Brooklyn Museum, 2009; Gift of Carol Siris Roaman, 1983 (2009.300.997)

At his most reductive, Halston created this caftan from a single length of fabric, cutting a hole for the head and leaving slits for the arms at the side seams. Like other French and American designers, Halston adopted the tie-dye technique, which typified clothing of the hippie generation, for his upscale fashions.

Evening Dress, ca. 1975

Purple silk crepe; label: "Halston"
Brooklyn Museum Costume Collection at The Metropolitan Museum of Art, Gift of the Brooklyn Museum, 2009; Gift of Alexandra A. Herzan from the Collection of Lily Auchincloss, 1996 (2009.300.600)

A classic example of Halston's minimalist aesthetic achieved through economy of construction, this toga-like dress is cut from a circular pattern. An interior elastic band holds it in place.

Evening Ensemble, ca. 1975

Apricot cashmere; label: "Halston/Made in Scotland"
Brooklyn Museum Costume Collection at The Metropolitan Museum of Art, Gift of the Brooklyn Museum, 2009; Gift of Alexandra A. Herzan from the Collection of Lily Auchincloss, 1996 (2009.300.2242a–c)

Halston's originality was in transforming the informality and comfort of sportswear into clothing suitable for all occasions. In this exemplar he rendered an elongated classic cardigan sweater and simple sleeveless sheath in luxurious Scottish cashmere to create what became one of his signature evening looks.

Geoffrey Beene

(American, 1927–2004)

Coat, ca. 1965

White wool gabardine printed with black, red, and blue; label: "Geoffrey Beene"
Brooklyn Museum Costume Collection at The Metropolitan Museum of Art, Gift of the Brooklyn Museum, 2009; Gift of Vivian Mook Baer in memory of Sylvia Terner Mook, 1983 (2009.300.545)

Beene asserted his interest in twentieth-century art in methods both subtle, as in regarding the body-garment relationship from artistic perspectives such as Cubism, and obvious, by preempting imagery. In 1962 the French painter and sculptor Jean Dubuffet (1901–1985) began a series painted exclusively in red, blue, white, and black, which this textile design references.

Evening Dress, ca. 1965

Purple and white printed silk, stylized leaf pattern
Brooklyn Museum Costume Collection at The Metropolitan Museum of Art, Gift of the Brooklyn Museum, 2009; Gift of Mrs. George Liberman, 1975 (2009.300.517)

The iconic leaf forms inspired by the late work of artist Henri Matisse (1869–1954), known as "cutouts," dominate this dress design. Beene echoes the curvilinear shapes in the low U-cut of the front bodice and the petal forms at the hem.

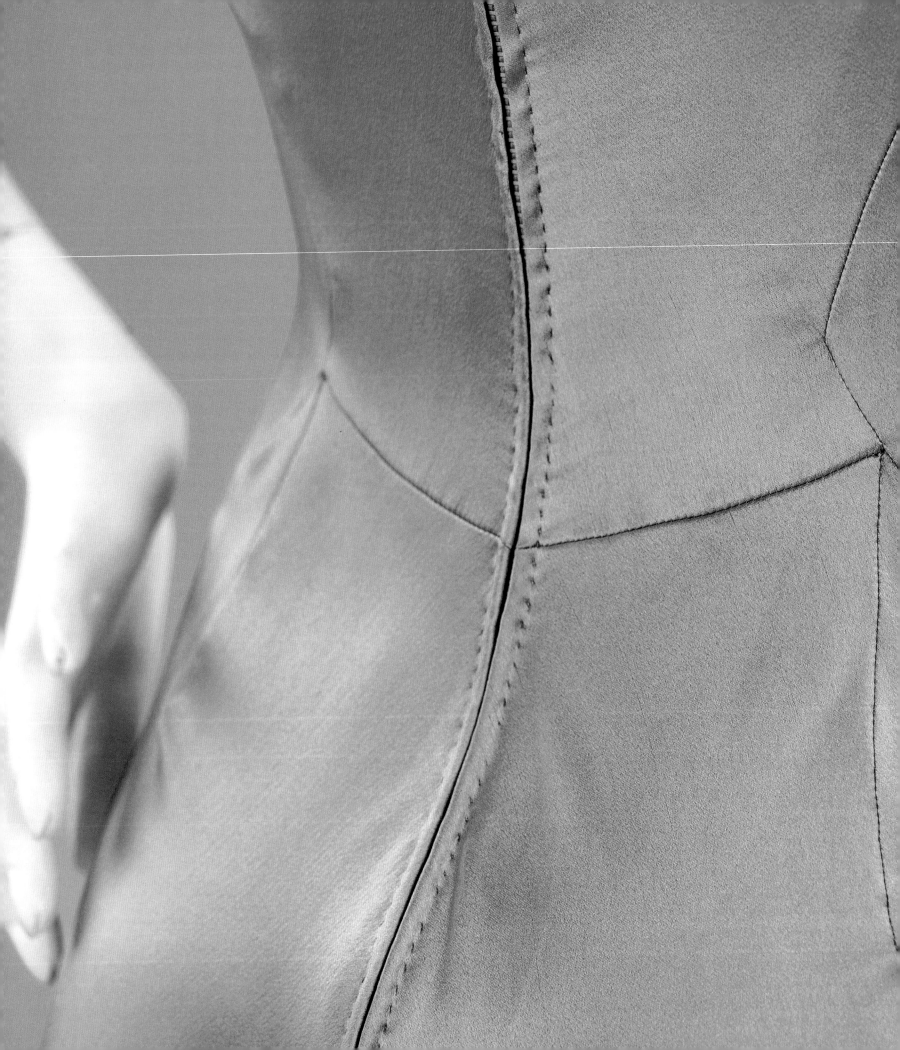

Charles James 1930s–1950s (active 1927–1978)

Charles James has achieved cult status in the field of fashion as much for his legacy of unforgettable clothes as for the magnetic force of his complex personality and the unorthodoxy of his creative process. Not having had formal dressmaking training, he developed his own methodology based on mathematical, architectural, and sculptural concepts as they related to the human body. His venturesome and wholly original approach to his work inspired and fascinated his contemporaries, as well as the generations of designers and admirers of his fashions who followed. Yet his name is not generally known today, because he was prominent for less than ten years, and, as James scholar Elizabeth Ann Coleman notes, his total output was fewer than one thousand garments over the nearly fifty years of his career.

A contemporary of American designers Adrian, Norell, and, on the other side of the Atlantic, Dior, James was born in 1906 in Surrey, England, of English and American parentage. His mother was from a socially prominent Chicago family, and his father a British military officer. He initiated his career in the late 1920s in Chicago and New York, but established his first couture business in London in the early 1930s. There he developed relationships with clients from the English aristocracy, as well as from American society, most notably style-setting heiress Millicent Huttleston Rogers, who would inspire and support him throughout her life. He also spent time with couturiers Poiret, Dior, Schiaparelli, and Balenciaga on his frequent trips to Paris, where they exchanged ideas and mutually influenced each other's work.

Although his heyday was in New York between 1947 to 1954, during the London years he developed key design elements and forms that he would use throughout his career—his wrap-over trouser skirt, body-hugging "Sirène" dress, spiral-cut and ribbon garments, and front point and pouf drapery, examples of which are illustrated here.

James moved to New York in 1940, and by 1945, after briefly designing for Elizabeth Arden, he had gained sufficient recognition to open an atelier at 699 Madison Avenue. From there he worked in the pure couture tradition, custom designing, fitting, and creating new forms for America's most prominent and stylish women, among them Millicent Rogers, art patron Dominique de Menil, Austine Hearst, journalist and wife of publisher William Randolph Hearst, Jr., and the entertainer Gypsy Rose Lee. Although his artistic perfectionism and personal demons led him to behave erratically and irresponsibly in all areas of his life, his clients clamored to be dressed by James and went to great lengths to support him artistically and financially.

In a 1957 letter accompanying a donation of funds to purchase, at James's request, several of his later evening gowns and his infant-wear collection for the Brooklyn Museum, Dominique de Menil wrote to Director Edgar C. Schenck: "My husband and I consider Charles James to be one of the most original and universal designers of this period and in this country. . . . Traveling as we do . . . we are amazed to see how many dresses from the Paris Couture actually can be traced back to Charles James."[1]

James's oeuvre is diverse and complex, the result of a restless creative force that was constantly pushing the boundaries of convention and of his own previous accomplishments. Because it took many forms with countless variations, his work is hard to characterize or classify. Some garments are elegant and timeless, while others are odd and controversial, having insectlike, vertebral, or other biomorphic features. Some incorporate the essence of modernity, while still others are updated versions of Victorian fashions.

One of James's credos was that there are a limited number of shapes and silhouettes but innumerable variations on them. He followed this tenet throughout his career by reusing and reworking forms and components once he had developed them, but always in different combinations that resulted in wholly new compositions. No matter what type of garment or shape he was creating, James used the female body as the point of reference rather than the defining factor of his formulation. Some of his designs cleave to the body, relying solely on cut, seams, and inventive ways of manipulating the fabric to achieve style and fit; others enhance and idealize its natural form with interior padding, corsetlike boning, and exterior drapery; and still others reshape the body into fantastic silhouettes that stand away from it. In these instances he used one of two methods as the primary way to achieve the effect—rigid, confining understructures, often modeled on Victorian prototypes such as the corset, bustle, and crinoline, or, conversely, perfectly calibrated cut, fabric choice, and variations in placement of grain and seams based on geometry. For these stand-away shapes, he considered the "air" between the body and the fabric to be the crucial design focus.[2] Within all of this diversity there are constants: James's sublime color sense, his artistry with combining fabrics having different surfaces and textures, and, foremost among them, the exhilarating tracery of his seams that follow the curves of the body, dissect it like a knife, or taper into infinity at the end of a dart.

Because they are the epitome of elegance and originality, as much sculpture as glamourous raiment, the incomparable evening dresses James produced between 1947 and 1954 are the designs for which he is best remembered.

Yet his tailored suits and more understated daywear are equal objects of admiration. In these, his methods of achieving precise fit and resolving volumetric and proportional challenges, as well as his seemingly endless variations on collars, lapels, and sleeves, are most apparent, further signifiers of the range and perfectionism of his art.

Drawn to the Brooklyn Museum's reputation for teaching and collecting objects to inspire new designs, James chose the museum as the primary place to document his career and to care for his legacy. He is thereby largely responsible for its definitive holdings of his work—nearly two hundred garments and six hundred related materials. His involvement with the Industrial Division, later to become the Design Lab, began in 1944 and continued until the late 1950s, during which

time he initiated numerous teaching and research projects. One of the earliest, begun in the mid-1940s, was a collaboration with Millicent Rogers, documenting through flat and sewn patterns the designs he had made for her in the previous ten years. The result was the inaugural exhibition in the Design Lab galleries, "A Decade of Design," showing primarily Rogers's James fashions and the patterns from which they were derived. In 1949 she donated much of this material—twenty-two garments and more than seventy-five patterns. Subsequent gifts from her sons included over fifty additional James fashions.

James himself donated four garments in 1947 and 1951, but mostly he used his prodigious powers of persuasion with his clients to amass at the museum what he referred to as the "corpus" of his work. The 1949 Rogers gift together with the exhibition established Brooklyn as the mecca for James material, giving him momentum to pursue funding for his various educational projects. In 1953, toward this end, he introduced his two other most influential clients, Austine Hearst and Dominique de Menil, to the museum.[3] Hearst's first gift, in 1953, consisted entirely of historical garments, mostly from the First Empire period, and the patterns James had drafted from them. Nine important James designs from her wardrobe followed in several donations made over the course of the 1960s, and she continued to gift works by other designers, as well as to offer financial and personal support to the Costume and Textile Department until her death in 1991. Dominique de Menil and her husband also supported James's efforts at documenting his work. They made several financial contributions between 1953 and 1958 to purchase garments designated by him as necessary to fill in gaps in the comprehensive holdings of his oeuvre. A final gift orchestrated by James was from members of the Ryerson family of Chicago, who purchased more than three hundred sketches from him for the collection in 1957.[4] Erik Lee Preminger's 1993 donation of twenty-four James garments worn by his mother, Gypsy Rose Lee, was the last significant addition to this extraordinarily rich trove.

Charles James

(American, born England, 1906–1978)

Evening Dress, 1936

Cream china silk brocaded with gold and silver
metallic leaf motif
Brooklyn Museum Costume Collection at The
Metropolitan Museum of Art, Gift of the Brooklyn
Museum, 2009; Gift of Mrs. Harrison Williams,
1948 (2009.300.687)

Front-point drapery is a signature James
form that he reiterated throughout the 1930s
and 1940s. The distinctive sculptural effect
of this early example contrasts with the
prevailing style for body-cleaving, bias-cut
styles typical of the period. The dress also
features an innovative halter bodice, which
appears to be wrapped spontaneously but is
in reality composed of five meticulously
joined pattern pieces. James rarely used
figured fabrics, preferring to give line and
form priority. However, by varying direc-
tions of the fabric's grain when cutting and
joining the pieces, he masterfully manipulated the leaf motif of this rare and expensive silk to emphasize the vertical and
diagonal bodice lines, while at the same
time creating the impression of random
patterning in the skirt, an impossibility
for a woven fabric.

Charles James

(American, born England, 1906–1978)

Dressing Gown, 1944

Pieced pink, yellow, gold, white, shell, and
tan silk satin ribbons
Brooklyn Museum Costume Collection at
The Metropolitan Museum of Art, Gift of
the Brooklyn Museum, 2009; Gift of
Edalgi Dinsha, 1944 (2009.300.674)

James's first ribbon garments were
fashioned from pre-World War I
6½-inch wide ribbons, which he
discovered in a Paris flea market,
made by the preeminent ribbon
manufacturer Colcombet of St.
Étienne. His affinity for ribbons
undoubtedly stemmed from his
early work as a milliner, but the
influential couturier Paul Poiret
purportedly suggested he design a
garment using them. This example
is similarly constructed of fine
6½-inch wide ribbons, uncut from
hem to shoulder. With mathematical precision, the ribbons are gradually tapered to accommodate the
fitted waist and then flared to provide amplitude over the bust. The
pointed hem reiterates the nature
of the ribbon materials, which are
usually finished with pointed ends.
One of three donated in 1944, this
was the first James garment to enter
the Brooklyn Museum collection.

Ball Gown, Spring 1947

Cream, yellow, and gray silk charmeuse; blue silk faille; gray and pale green silk taffeta
Formerly collection of Millicent Huttleston Rogers
Brooklyn Museum Costume Collection at The Metropolitan Museum of Art, Gift of the Brooklyn Museum, 2009; Gift of Arturo and Paul Peralta-Ramos, 1954 (2009.300.1187)

Alternating sections of supple gleaming charmeuse, crisp shimmering taffeta, and stiff matte faille determine the shape, movement, and visual appeal of this ball gown. Elaborating on the concept of his early ribbon garments, James used lengths of fabric to construct the skirt of this dress. The variance in weight, drape, and light-reflective properties add multidimensional effects to a dress meant for motion. The vanishing-point taper of the gores from hem to waist back exemplify James's virtuoso seaming techniques and affinity for attenuated forms.

Charles James

(American, born England, 1906–1978)

"La Sirène" Evening Dress, 1941

Black silk crepe
Brooklyn Museum Costume Collection at The
Metropolitan Museum of Art, Gift of the Brooklyn
Museum, 2009; Bequest of Marta C. Raymond, 1989
(2009.300.576)

Transcending the styles of three decades,
James produced this dress, one of his most
popular designs, from the late 1930s to the
mid-1950s. While its lines correspond to the
slinky silhouettes of glamourous 1930s fashions, it parts company with the bias-cut
sheaths of that decade in cut, construction,
and attitude. The tapered front spinelike element, supporting proportionally spaced
upward tucks, adds an edgy anatomical feature, ambiguously suggestive of crustacean,
reptilian, or human skeletal forms, a signature
James conceit.

Evening Dress, 1946

Black silk velvet; cranberry silk satin; chocolate brown silk faille; black wool-backed silk crepe
Formerly collection of Millicent Huttleston Rogers
Brooklyn Museum Costume Collection at The Metropolitan Museum of Art, Gift of the Brooklyn Museum, 2009; Gift of Arturo and Paul Peralta-Ramos, 1954 (2009.300.795)

It was a James innovation to piece together contrasting fabrics such as satin, faille, and taffeta in one garment, as he has done here and in the dress illustrated on page 163. Ambiguity, another signature element of his design concepts, is also a compelling feature of this sculptural form. Its construction reconfigures the body by thrusting the front forward with stiff silk faille and satin in winglike curves at the hips, leaving the softer crepe draped over the back, a reversal of the norm in which the weight of construction is placed at the back of the body.

Jerry Cooke (American, 1921–2005) and Claude Huston. Evening dresses by Charles James modeled in his showroom. *Collier's*, September 20, 1947, p. 100.
©Crowell-Collier Publishing Co., Springfield, Ohio

Bernard Boutet de Monvel (French, 1881–1949). *Millicent Rogers (Dress by Charles James)*, 1949. Oil on canvas. 85 x 69 cm. Courtesy of Mrs. Peter Salm and Barry Friedman Ltd., New York

Charles James
(American, born England, 1906–1978)

Evening Dress, 1947

Ivory silk duchesse satin; handwritten
label: "Ch. James/'47"
Formerly collection of Millicent Huttleston
Rogers
Brooklyn Museum Costume Collection at
The Metropolitan Museum of Art, Gift of
the Brooklyn Museum, 2009; Gift of
Arturo and Paul Peralta-Ramos, 1954
(2009.300.1861)

Draping fabric into sculptural
poufs was a technique James
worked with throughout his career.
Knee-level poufs inspired by the
pannier drapery of the 1912–14
period were among several variations that he favored. Although
seemingly spontaneous, the folds
are carefully planned and controlled
by way of construction and understructure. While some examples
have heavier padding or interlining,
the pouf here is lightly supported
at the sides with net, leaving the
center free. Like three-dimensional
sculpture, the dress has a different
appearance from every angle. It
was worn by Millicent Rogers in
a portrait by the artist Bernard
Boutet de Monvel (opposite).

Charles James
(American, born England, 1906–1978)

Evening Dress, 1945

Peach crepe-back silk satin
Formerly collection of Millicent Huttleston Rogers
Brooklyn Museum Costume Collection at The
Metropolitan Museum of Art, Gift of the Brooklyn
Museum, 2009; Gift of Arturo and Paul
Peralta-Ramos, 1954 (2009.300.2787)

The intersection of flawless cut, unconventional seams, sexual symbolism, artful draping, and luscious color define this as an iconic example of James's work. In celebration of the female body, the bodice is fitted with diagonal seams that meet long bust darts in breathtaking points at the pelvic bones, calling attention to the reproductive organs they protect. Projecting cartridge pleats gather the fabric into the skirt's graceful front drapery at the same point. The drapery reasserts itself at the shoulders, with a seemingly impossible abundance of folds emanating from the fitted bust. Attesting to James's abrogation of the dressmaker's side seams, right and left torso pattern pieces wrap to the back and form points that facilitate fit and add decorative interest (see p. 158).

Charles James evening dress in Modess advertisement. *Harper's Bazaar*, April 1950, p. 178.
Courtesy of *Harper's Bazaar*, Hearst Communications, Inc. © 2010

Erwin Blumenfeld (American, 1897–1969). Evening dress
by Charles James. *Vogue*, April 15, 1947, p. 123. Erwin
Blumenfeld/Condé Nast Archive, © Condé Nast
Publications

Gene Fenn (American, 1911–2001). Millicent Rogers wearing an evening dress by Charles James. *Town & Country*, July 1948, p. 39. Courtesy of *Town & Country*, Hearst Communications, Inc. © 2010

Charles James

(American, born England, 1906–1978)

Ball Gown, 1948

Peach silk faille; marigold taffeta; label: "Charles James/'48"
Formerly collection of Millicent Huttleston Rogers
Brooklyn Museum Costume Collection at The Metropolitan
Museum of Art, Gift of the Brooklyn Museum, 2009; Gift of
Arturo and Paul Peralta-Ramos, 1954 (54.141.94)

The elegance of the eighteenth-century open robe
and petticoat and James's fascination with sexuality
and procreation merge in this design, which alludes
to female genitalia, not unlike the flower paintings of
Georgia O'Keeffe (1887–1986), whose first New York
retrospective exhibition was held at the Museum of
Modern Art in 1946. A more subliminal reference
to the eighteenth-century art of seduction cultivated
by the upper classes may also be at play. Brooklyn
Museum records document this gown as a collaborative effort between James and Millicent Rogers,
who is said to have suggested the design and fabric
for the underskirt.

Charles James
(American, born England, 1906–1978)

Evening Dress, 1948

Black silk satin and velvet
Brooklyn Museum Costume Collection at The Metropolitan
Museum of Art, Gift of the Brooklyn Museum, 2009; Gift of
Millicent Huttleston Rogers, 1949 (2009.300.734)

In this supremely sophisticated construction, the
casual, unstructured bib-front bodice, barely held to
the body by straps crisscrossing at back, contrasts with
the formidable volume and formality of the skirt. The
pannier drapery favored by James is here at the back,
in comparison to others where it is concentrated in the
front. A touch of black velvet at the lower back and
waist is a quintessential James refinement.

Fritz Henle (American, born
Germany, 1909–1993). Evening
dress by Charles James (detail).
Holiday, January 1949, p. 121.
© The Curtis Publishing Co.,
Philadelphia, Pennsylvania

Ball Gown, 1951

Ivory silk satin
Brooklyn Museum Costume Collection at The Metropolitan Museum of
Art, Gift of the Brooklyn Museum, 2009; Gift of Mr. and Mrs. Robert
Coulson, 1964 (2009.300.1311)

The quadrant was a mathematical concept that James worked
with throughout his career. Here it is represented in four poufs
that reconfigure the body into a fantasy shape reminiscent of
Victorian polonaise drapery, or the popular settees known as
"puffs." It has the air of perfectly proportioned timeless elegance
for which James's evening wear of the late 1940s and early 1950s
was admired. James used diverse methods to support his shapes.
This gown is lightly supported with a tarlatan interfacing. The
donor wore it to her debutante party and later to the Eisenhower
Inaugural Ball in 1953.

Louise Dahl-Wolfe
(American, 1895–1989).
Evening dress by Charles
James (detail). *Harper's
Bazaar*, December 1948,
p. 104. Courtesy of
Harper's Bazaar, Hearst
Communications, Inc.
© 2010

Charles James
(American, born England, 1906–1978)

Dress, 1950

Rose and black pin-striped taffeta
Formerly collection of Millicent
Huttleston Rogers
Brooklyn Museum Costume Collection at
The Metropolitan Museum of Art, Gift of
the Brooklyn Museum, 2009; Gift of
Arturo and Paul Peralta-Ramos, 1954
(2009.300.180)

One of James's first designs was a
dress that spiraled around the body
with a zipper closure. He focused
on other ideas in the 1940s, but
returned to the spiral in the early
1950s. The same sense of movement
is captured in this bodice, which is
constructed in two off-grain fabric
pieces, which incorporate the sleeves
and twist around, rather than conform to, the shape of the body. A
short diagonal zipper at the left
front neckline emphasizes the spiral
effect. In an integral concept that
merges fabric and cut, the change-
able nature of the striped silk,
which was a specific fabric used in
men's coat linings, exploits the
dynamics of light to enhance the
energetic cut.

Dinner Suit, 1950

Light brown silk satin; black silk velvet; *changeante* violet silk taffeta lining
Brooklyn Museum Costume Collection at The Metropolitan Museum of Art, Gift of the Brooklyn Museum, 2009; Gift of Jerome K. Orbach, 1954 (2009.300.195a, b)

The arc sleeve is probably James's most heralded sleeve shape. Worked out with a compass, the remarkable construction features a seam that arcs from the sleeve end to the front side waist of the bodice, elucidating their integral cut. The fullness and curves of the sleeves give an overall rounded form to the bodice, a derivation of the 1830s Romantic style. The bodice is paired with a skirt that is rounded at front and straight at back, where two modernistic finlike flanges protrude from each side. This mix of unorthodox shapes reconfigures the human body into a more biomorphic than anthropomorphic form.

Charles James
(American, born England, 1906–1978)

Dress, 1952

Gray silk faille
Brooklyn Museum Costume Collection at The Metropolitan Museum of Art, Gift of the Brooklyn Museum, 2009; Gift of Muriel Bultman Francis, 1967 (2009.300.450a, b)

Always experimenting with contrasts of fit and volume, James molded the bodice front of this cocktail dress to the body with long vertical bust darts, and left the back full to fall into a pleat secured at the waist. Conversely, the skirt front has a structured cantilevered hip yoke that causes it to stand away from the body, while the back is seamed to fit snugly over the hips until liberated by the loose drape of a center box pleat, giving swing to the back.

Ensemble, 1947

Garnet wool broadcloth; pink silk satin lining
Brooklyn Museum Costume Collection at The Metropolitan Museum of Art, Gift of the Brooklyn Museum, 2009; Gift of Mrs. William Randolph Hearst, Jr., 1960 (2009.300.1278a–c)

An example of James's refined tailoring techniques, this suit was one of the donor's favorite garments. In a letter that accompanied the gift, now in the Brooklyn Museum Library Archives, she wrote that it provided her with the freedom she needed for frequent international travel. The ensemble consists of a short skirt for day and a long culotte skirt, which James referred to as his "wrap-over trouser skirt," for evening. Similar to a figure eight, this innovative design wrapped one leg like a trouser and crossed over in front to cover the other. James first showed it in 1939.

Charles James

(American, born England, 1906–1978)

Coat, ca. 1950

Camel tan wool vicuña; dark violet silk satin lining
Brooklyn Museum Costume Collection at The Metropolitan Museum of Art,
Gift of the Brooklyn Museum, 2009; Gift of Muriel Bultman Francis, 1968
(2009.300.462)

The cocoon, a symbol of metamorphosis and rebirth, is a form
James used throughout his career. In this rendition, a diminutive
funnel collar elongates and narrows the neck, contrasting with
the enveloping volume of the coat's body. Outsized buttons and
cuffs correspond to the exaggerated volume, adding proportional
harmony to the form.

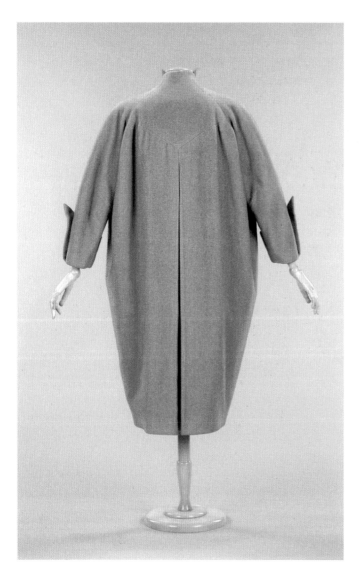

Coat, 1954

Red brushed wool; apricot silk satin lining
Brooklyn Museum Costume Collection at The Metropolitan
Museum of Art, Gift of the Brooklyn Museum, 2009; Gift
of Mrs. William Randolph Hearst, Jr., 1960 (2009.300.274)

James's coat designs of the early 1950s elucidate
most clearly his mastery of line and cut. With
mathematical precision, he quartered the torso in
this example, which the donor, Austine Hearst,
identified as the first of his Empire-line coats and
the forerunner of the sack, first shown in Paris in
1955. The tight fit of the upper bodice, molded and
padded over the bust, and the loose fall of the
back both emanate from the same horizontal line
through the bust. It is one of the challenging construction techniques James used to change the
proportions and the shape of the body. The coat
is lined in stunning apricot satin.

Charles James made versions of this dress for numerous prominent clients, among them Millicent Rogers, Barbara (Babe) Paley, Gypsy Rose Lee, Austine Hearst, and Dominique de Menil. In a characteristically grand gesture, he organized a finale at a March of Dimes Benefit Ball in the early 1950s, in which eight of them appeared with tuxedoed escorts carrying bouquets that matched the dress. The design epitomizes James's talent for combining materials with varying textures and surfaces that respond differently to light and movement. An asymmetrical drape of luminous satin contrasts with the rich velvet of the bodice, while pleated organdy flounces add crispness and texture.

John Rawlings (American, 1912–1970).
Mrs. William S. Paley wearing an evening dress by Charles James (detail). *Vogue*, November 1, 1950, pp. 114–15. John Rawlings/Condé Nast Archive, ©Condé Nast Publications

Charles James
(American, born England, 1906–1978)

Ball Gown, 1949–50

Ruby red silk velvet, satin and red pleated
taffeta
Brooklyn Museum Costume Collection at
The Metropolitan Museum of Art, Gift of the
Brooklyn Museum, 2009; Gift of Erik Lee
Preminger in memory of his mother, Gypsy
Rose Lee, 1993 (2009.300.585a–d)

This example (left) has two flounces,
one white organdy, and the other is
red pleated taffeta, illustrated on the
opposite page.

Ball Gown, 1949–50

Ruby red silk velvet, satin, and white pleated
organdy
Formerly collection of Millicent Huttleston
Rogers
Brooklyn Museum Costume Collection at
The Metropolitan Museum of Art, Gift of the
Brooklyn Museum, 2009; Gift of Arturo and
Paul Peralta-Ramos, 1954 (2009.300.2786)

Charles James
(American, born England, 1906–1978)

"Four Leaf Clover" Ball Gown, 1953

Ivory duchesse silk satin; ivory silk faille; black velvet (*velours de Lyon*)
Brooklyn Museum Costume Collection at The Metropolitan Museum of Art, Gift of the Brooklyn Museum, 2009; Gift of Mrs. Cornelius V. Whitney, 1953 (2009.300.779)

While James's inspiration for this dress was likely the 1860s silhouette supported by a cage crinoline, its construction is far more complex than its precursor made of concentric steel wires connected by linen tapes. This one was built using two separate understructures of boning and stiff interfacings to give it shape and balance. The fifteen-pound skirt was engineered to rest comfortably on the hips, and, unlike the cage crinoline, to effectuate a graceful glide rather than a back and forth sway. With artistic bravado, James heightened the visual drama by separating the luminosity of ivory satin and the muted reflectivity of ivory faille on the upper and lower sections with a curvaceous black velvet swath, which further defines the serpentine effect of the four-lobed skirt. As he considered himself to be a sculptor, engineer, and architect, James thought this design his greatest achievement.

The original version was made for Austine Hearst to wear to the Eisenhower Inaugural Ball in January 1953, but it was not completed in time. She was, however, able to wear it to the coronation ball in London in June. This example is a duplicate made for the donor, Eleanor Searle Whitney, soon after the original for Mrs. Hearst was completed.

Charles James

(American, born England, 1906–1978)

"Swan" Ball Gown, 1953

Black silk chiffon; pale pink silk satin; black, pink, rose and oyster white tulle; label: "an original design by Charles James" Brooklyn Museum Costume Collection at The Metropolitan Museum of Art, Gift of the Brooklyn Museum, 2009; Gift of Rodman A. Heeren, 1961 (2009.300.849)

Borrowing from the Victorians, James interpreted the 1870s bustle dress in construction, form, and decoration to render his swan silhouette. A hollow double-lobed understructure at back, corresponding to a period bustle, and similar foundations over the hips cause the derrière and hips to extend beyond the natural form. Like the bustle, a divided effect at back emphasizes the round form of the buttocks and at the same time suggests the back of a swan, with wings folded gracefully on its back. The apron-front drapery is also a borrowing from 1870s styles.

Charles James
(American, born England, 1906–1978)

"Tree" Ball Gown, 1955

Rose pink silk taffeta; white silk satin;
red, pink, and white tulle; label (skirt):
"an original design by Charles James";
handwritten label (bodice): "Charles
James/'55"
Brooklyn Museum Costume Collection at
The Metropolitan Museum of Art, Gift of
the Brooklyn Museum, 2009; Gift of Mrs.
Douglas Fairbanks, Jr., 1981 (2009.300.991)

Reshaping the body through corse-
try was one of James's lifelong
fascinations. The quintessential
feminine shape is perfected in this
dress through rigid interior boning
in the bodice and intricately tucked
exterior hip drapery. As an added
touch of sheer romanticism, the
bouffant skirt is faced with rich
white satin and supported by a profusion of colored tulle, a hidden
blossom made visible with movement. Deploying a double entendre,
James named the design for one
of his clients, Marietta Peabody
Fitzgerald Tree, mother of the
model Penelope Tree, and also as a
reference to the plant form, which
the silhouette, uprooted, resembles.

Charles James
(American, born England, 1906–1978)

"Butterfly" Ball Gown, 1955

Smoke gray silk chiffon; pale gray silk satin; aubergine,
lavender, and oyster white tulle; label: "an original design by
Charles James"
Brooklyn Museum Costume Collection at The Metropolitan
Museum of Art, Gift of the Brooklyn Museum, 2009; Gift of
Mrs. John de Menil, 1957 (2009.300.816)

Victorian, surreal, seductive, modern, this tightly
fitted sheath with an exuberant explosion of multicolored tulle invites multiple interpretations. The
form alludes to the extreme bustle of the 1880s,
which swayed seductively with the wearer's move-
ments. At the same time, it is, as the name implies,
a butterfly form that has morphed the female body
into that of an insect with iridescent wings, which
shimmer with movement. The curvaceous satin
side flanges serve both to heighten the eroticism of
feminine curves and to underscore the wing motif.
References to the past aside, it was a form hitherto
unknown in the history of fashion, giving it modernist status. The dress weighs eighteen pounds;
twenty-five yards of tulle were used in its making.

Charles James
(American, born England, 1906–1978)

Evening Dress, ca. 1960

Light beige silk satin, taupe silk faille, brown silk chiffon
Brooklyn Museum Costume Collection at The Metropolitan Museum of
Art, Gift of the Brooklyn Museum, 2009; Gift of Erik Lee Preminger in
memory of his mother, Gypsy Rose Lee, 1993 (2009.300.589)

James designed with the philosophy that there were relatively
few basic forms but an infinite number of variations on them.
He therefore routinely created original fashions by reworking
and combining previously developed elements. In this version
of his "Diamond" dress made for the entertainer Gypsy Rose
Lee, he added the sleeve treatment of what he called his
"Rose" bodice to the "Diamond" dress skirt (facing page) and
substituted side gathers for the arc form at the skirt top to
create a customized garment.

Gypsy Rose Lee wearing an evening dress by Charles James in a Smirnoff advertisement. *Life*, November 9, 1962, p. 69. © Ste, Pierre Smirnoff Fls. (Division of
Heublein) Hartford, Conn., 1962

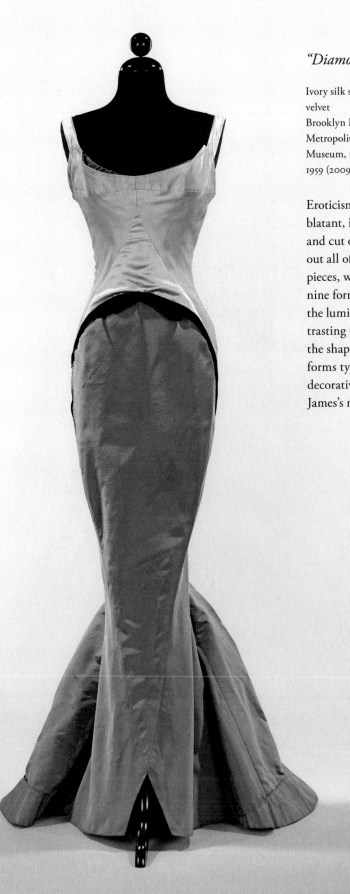

"Diamond" Evening Dress, 1957

Ivory silk satin; beige faille (*gros de londres*); black silk velvet
Brooklyn Museum Costume Collection at The Metropolitan Museum of Art, Gift of the Brooklyn Museum, 2009; Gift of Mr. and Mrs. John de Menil, 1959 (2009.300.832)

Eroticism takes many forms, both subtle and blatant, in James's oeuvre. In the design and cut of this mermaid-like dress he pulled out all of the stops. Curvaceous pattern pieces, which abstract and idealize the feminine form, are accentuated by playing off the luminescent and matte textures of contrasting materials. Black velvet reiterates the shapes. An affinity for the biomorphic forms typical of 1950s architectural and decorative arts aesthetics is evidence of James's modernity.

Winglike forms feature prominently in James's designs. He developed the first of his feather fans in 1935 and used them to accessorize his dresses in numerous magazine fashion spreads in the late 1940s.

Charles James
(American, born England, 1906–1978

Fan, 1935–47

Feather
Brooklyn Museum Costume Collection at The Metropolitan Museum of Art, Gift of the Brooklyn Museum, 2009; Brooklyn Museum Collection (2009.300.1245)

Fan, 1935–47

Feather
Brooklyn Museum Costume Collection at The Metropolitan Museum of Art, Gift of the Brooklyn Museum, 2009; Brooklyn Museum Collection (2009.300.2244)

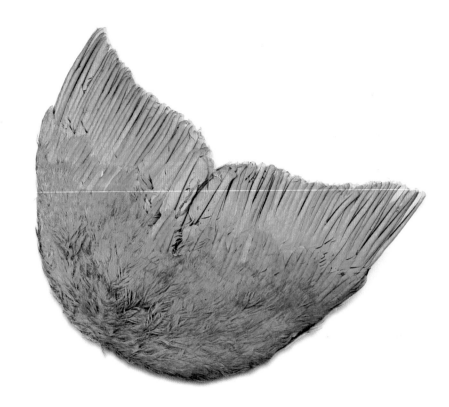

"Matador" Hat, 1948

Black silk velvet and satin; label: "Charles James/699 Madison Avenue/New York"
Brooklyn Museum Costume Collection at The Metropolitan Museum of Art, Gift of the Brooklyn Museum, 2009; Gift of Clare Mallison Langdon, 1969 (2009.300.2149 a–c)

A rare example of extant James millinery, this interpretation of a matador's beret-like hat is constructed in quadrants that are defined by seaming in the dome, as well as by satin ribbons over the brim. James scholar Elizabeth Ann Coleman ascertained that this hat was one of the designer's inspirations for his "Four Leaf Clover" gown. In a skillful manipulation of fabric, the brim velvet is braided and shirred.

The hat box below is original to the hat and was part of the gift. There are very few in existence. The elegant numbers with tapered ends evince James's affinity for attenuated forms, while the repetition of his name around the perimeter establishes a sense of motion consistent with the inherent dynamism of his designs.

Rarities 1600s–1960s

The objects in this chapter are designated as rarities because of the distinctive qualities that set them apart from other fine examples of their types. Although they do not for the most part come from the collection categories set out in these chapters, they are of such importance that this book of masterworks would be diminished without their inclusion. Some are extraordinary because of their sheer beauty and the technical virtuosity involved in making them, others for the fascinating cultural narratives that are associated with them. A number incorporate both qualities. Regardless, each carries with it an intensified power to engage, delight, and inspire further inquiry into the myriad areas of interest that surround them. In short, they have what might be called the "wow factor."

The pieces share little in common aside from their star quality. They come from diverse museological categories of the collection—womenswear, menswear, outerwear, and accessories. Within those broad categories there are rare laces, traditional folk dress, and clothing associated with film, royalty, and the military.

Costumes for film or theater are not usually acquired by art museum curators unless there are ameliorating factors, such as connections with the fashion world. The evening dress worn by Ava Gardner in *The Barefoot Contessa* was made for her by the Fontana sisters, whose Italian couture house was closely associated with glamorous designs for movie stars. As the aesthetic of their on-screen and off-screen creations did not vary significantly, the dress stands on its own merit as a fine example of Fontana craft and the quintessence of fifties style. Its striking presence in the film amplifies its capacity to delight. The commercial version of Scarlett O'Hara's hat from *Gone with the Wind* shares the same fashion scenario as the Fontana dress, with an added point of interest. Although costumes for *Gone with the Wind* were the creations of the great Hollywood costume designer Walter Plunkett, the film's producers hired John P. John, one of America's top milliners, to design the hats. He did not capitalize on his film work commercially,

however, because the hat wholesaler Kartiganer and Company negotiated a contract with MGM not only to reproduce *Gone with the Wind* hat styles but also to use John P. John's company name, John Frederics, Inc., on the label.[1] Regardless of its maker, the true power of the hat is its iconic status as a player in one of the most memorable scenes of what is among the greatest and certainly most popular films of the twentieth century.

The two outfits made by John Cavanagh and Simonetta et Fabiani have a different association with the film industry. As part of a 1960s promotional project that tapped the creative talents of some of the era's most prominent designers by asking them to prophesy the styles of the future, the garments tell an engaging story in which the film, fashion, and museum worlds collaborate. As well-crafted and thoughtfully conceived outfits, they are also bona fide examples of 1960s designer clothing eminently suited for a place in a fashion collection.

While Anna May Wong's dress by the costume designer Travis Banton lacks the fashion connection, it exemplifies 1930s glamour, which was largely fueled by the costumes of Hollywood stars. Its dazzling sequined motifs qualify it for extraordinary status in any arena. On another level, as the dragon motif embodies Anna May Wong's stereotypical casting as the evil "Dragon Lady," the dress invites inquiry into the riveting story of her career-long struggle with discrimination.

Of the three items connected to royalty, the court dress Emily Warren Roebling wore in the presence of the queen of England and the czar and czarina of Russia represents all of the opulence and grandeur that such associations bring to mind. While, as a likely Worth creation, it could be presented in the second chapter of this publication, the provenance linked to the building of the Brooklyn Bridge and the detailed rendering of the dress in a Carolus-Duran portrait elevate it to rarity status. The other two pieces, coincidentally belonging to the queen of England and the czar of Russia, while beautifully made, have an impact of intimacy rather than grandeur. The dress worn by Queen Victoria in a family photograph taken at the christening of her great-grandchild, Prince Edward Albert of York, born in June 1894, is equipped with four functional pockets and is of a suitably light weight for the summer weather. Its unpretentiousness matches the queen's relaxed posture and maternal gaze as she holds the infant. Similarly, seen alone minus the outer finery that usually covered it, the shirt belonging to Nicholas II, the last czar of Russia, evokes the human side of the royal persona. Its embroidered cipher, as well as the cleverly hidden label of the company that supplied him with sartorial necessities worn closest to the body, reinforce this impression.

These items came to the Brooklyn Museum in various ways—some as single items, some as purchases, others as parts of larger collections. The dress purchased in 1922 represents the museum's early interest in lace collecting, which began in 1915. Although lace was a focus in the early years, an important collection containing many of the most valuable examples, such as the seventeenth-century collar in this section, was acquired in 1966. Regional headwear from France and Russia are included as signifiers of the important holdings of traditional clothing from Eastern and Western Europe that are part of the collection. Finally, as an example of the many donations associated with the Design Lab's influence, the 1960s fashion prophesy project is a playful reminder of the Design Lab's sponsorship of creative activities related to the fashion and design industries.

Italian or British

Collar, 1675–1700

Cream needle-made linen lace, gros point type
Brooklyn Museum Costume Collection at The Metropolitan Museum of Art, Gift of the Brooklyn Museum, 2009; Gift of the executors of the estate of Clara M. Blum in memory of Mr. and Mrs. Albert Blum, 1966 (2009.300.2055)

Incorporated in the overall floral and foliate pattern of this lace collar are two female figures at either side (top), the initials "AC" at the left shoulder, various creatures at the center back point, and, at mid-center back (measuring less than one inch high), a freestanding, three-dimensional female figure in period costume with black silk eyes and fully formed front and back (bottom).

The extravagant variety of fillings (patterned interior areas of the motif), the superimposition of floral motifs over them, and the elaborate embellishment of the brides (connecting threads) in this design indicate a technical virtuosity far beyond the norm for gros point lace. Since the incorporation of three-dimensional figures is common in English embroidery of the same date, a British attribution is considered.

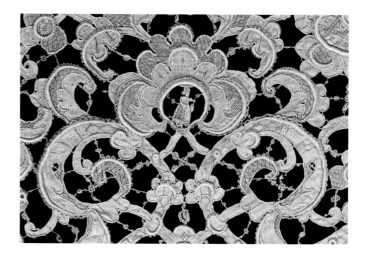

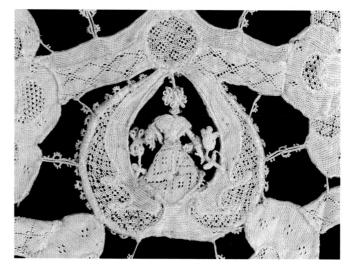

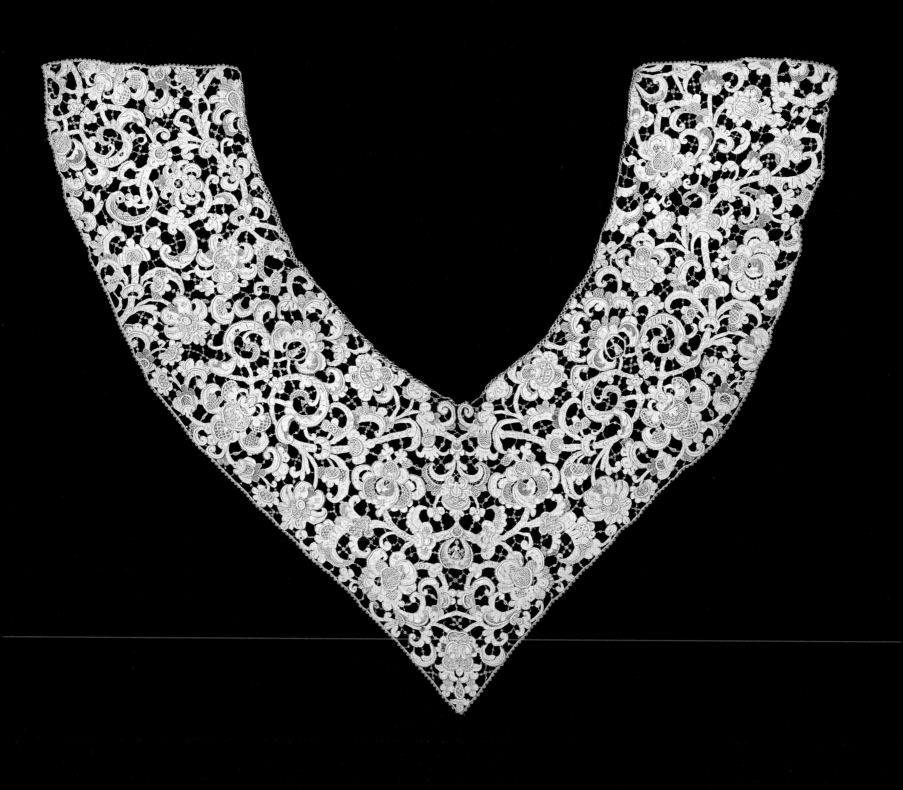

European

Wedding Dress, ca. 1870

Cream crochet cotton lace, Irish type
Brooklyn Museum Costume Collection
at The Metropolitan Museum of Art,
Gift of the Brooklyn Museum, 2009;
Ella C. Woodward Memorial Fund, 1922
(2009.300.1664)

Three-dimensional motifs, including
roses, lilies of the valley, hanging
fuchsias, morning glories, buds, and
berries, interspersed among flat
and folded leaves and ferns, animate
the surface of this extraordinary lace
dress. The naturalistic rendering
and intricacy of the work set this
apart from the ubiquitous formulaic
designs typical of Irish crochet lace.

British

Morning Gown, ca. 1825

Multicolored roller-printed plain weave cotton, diamond-shaped piecing
Brooklyn Museum Costume Collection at The Metropolitan Museum of Art, Gift of the Brooklyn Museum, 2009; Purchase, Designated Purchase Fund, 1983 (2009.300.999)

Morning gowns, also known as banyans, were a type of primarily male attire worn before formally dressing for the day. Dating from the seventeenth century, most, but not all, were unfitted flowing robes made from patterned silks or printed cottons that had a vaguely "exotic" connotation. This one, from a later date, is tailored according to the period's fashionable male silhouette with puffed shoulders, high collar, fitted bodice, and full skirt gathered at back. Composed of hundreds of diamond-shaped swatches of printed cotton pieced together like a quilt top, the fabric was undoubtedly worked at home by family members, but the gown's complex construction likely required the expertise of a professional tailor.

Antony Berrus
(French, 1815–1883)

or

Amédée Couder
(French, 1797–1864)

Shawl, ca. 1855

Polychrome wool-wrapped silk
Brooklyn Museum Costume Collection at The Metropolitan Museum of Art, Gift of
the Brooklyn Museum, 2009; Gift of The Roebling Society, 1985 (2009.300.2212)

Large rectangular patterned shawls, generally referred to as "paisleys,"
were an important fashion accessory worn over the wide crinoline skirts
of the 1850s and 1860s. Mid-century advances in the Jacquard punch-
card weaving system that created them led to virtuosic examples conceived as exhibition pieces rather than for wear. The style and extreme
complexity of this one suggest an attribution to either of the two most
prominent mid-nineteenth-century French shawl designers. Woven in
end-to-end mirror image, the complex chinoiserie design is centered with
a water scene populated by fanciful creatures, exotic vegetation, and
mythological figures astride flying fish and dragons. Pavilion scenes,
depicting a double staircase leading to an arched entrance inhabited by
a peacock, flank the central motif.

Lafarge
(French)

Parasol, 1890–99

Black and white silk chiffon; wood; metal; marble; enamel

Brooklyn Museum Costume Collection at The Metropolitan Museum of Art, Gift of the Brooklyn Museum, 2009; Gift of Gifford B. Pinchot, 1961 (2009.300.2497)

Shirred silk chiffon was commonly used in fashions of the 1890s. Here it forms the exterior and interior of the parasol's canopy. Ensuring that it be a thing of beauty from any angle, each rib and stretcher is similarly covered, a labor-intensive task requiring specialized skill. Completing the luxurious effect is its marble handle with silver overlay and enamel work.

Betaille
(French)

Parasol, 1900–1910

Black and white striped silk taffeta, chiné satin border; wood; metal; leather; quartz; glass; enamel; tortoiseshell
Brooklyn Museum Costume Collection at The Metropolitan Museum of Art, Gift of the Brooklyn Museum, 2009; Gift of Mrs. Alan L. Corey, Jr., Mrs. Arnold Newbold, and Mrs. Augustus Paine, in memory of their mother, Mrs. William Russell Grace, 1980 (2009.300.2191a–b)

Parasols were an essential decorative and functional accessory for the daytime toilettes of the Belle Époque woman. The essence of French artistry, this one is an ultimate expression of the ornamental possibilities of the parasol, as well as the adoration of pets. Whimsical yet regal in its fabrication, an amethyst French bulldog with green eyes set in 14-karat gold and sporting a pearl collar surmounts the handle, protected when not on view by a custom-fitted leather jewelry case lined in white kid.

The artistry and luxury are carried through every detail of the parasol design. The striped taffeta of the canopy is woven with a contrasting satin-weave warp-print border; the ribs and stretchers (not visible) are individually covered with the canopy taffeta; the decorative fittings are 14-karat gold; the rib tips are covered with material matching the tortoiseshell handle; and the amethyst color is picked up in the border flowers.

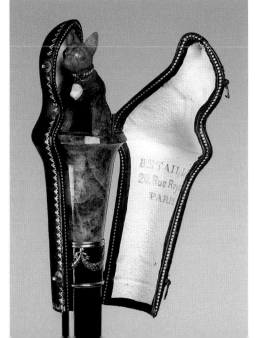

Attributed to Jean-Philippe Worth
(French, 1856–1926)

Court Presentation Ensemble, 1896

Yellow silk satin; white silk satin with gold and silver metal thread embroidery, Baroque floral and vine pattern; ecru embroidered net lace; yellow silk chiffon; yellow satin picoté ribbon; violet velvet; silk crepe and velvet orchids; lavender silk tulle
Brooklyn Museum Costume Collection at The Metropolitan Museum of Art, Gift of the Brooklyn Museum, 2009; Anonymous gift in memory of Mrs. John Roebling, 1970 (2009.300.941a–e)

Emily Warren Roebling (1843–1903) wore this gown for her formal presentation to British monarch Queen Victoria at the Court of St. James in 1896 and on May 14 of the same year to the coronation of the czar and czarina (Nicholas II and Alexandra Fyodorovna) of Russia. Emily was the wife of Washington Augustus Roebling (1837–1926), son of John R. Roebling (1806–1869), designer of the Brooklyn Bridge. Washington became chief engineer after his father's death. When Washington developed caisson disease, preventing his further physical involvement, Emily Roebling took over the on-site supervision of the project, ensuring her husband's ability to remain in charge despite his illness until the bridge was completed in 1883.

Presentation at court was an important event coveted by men and women in the upper echelons of American and European society. Court protocol set sartorial requirements related to headwear, decorative materials, and, most significantly, long trains that required the assistance of attendants to maneuver. The trains, worn at either the waist or at the shoulder, were removable after the official presentation.

Allusions in this dress to other historical eras, evident in the Renaissance-style sleeves and the skirt style similar to that of the eighteenth-century *robe à la française*, as well as the opulent silver and gold embroidery on the bodice, convey the aura of grandeur requisite for being in the presence of royalty. The velvet train strewn with exquisite silk orchids heightens the effect. While the ensemble does not bear a Worth label, the hallmarks of fine workmanship, luxurious textiles, historical references, and uncommon color combinations verify the attribution. Completing a rare confluence of important history, fashion, and art, Charles-Émile-Auguste Carolus-Duran (1838–1917) painted a portrait of Emily Roebling wearing the dress; the portrait is in the collection of the Brooklyn Museum.

Charles-Émile-Auguste Carolus-Duran (French, 1838–1917). *Portrait of Emily Warren Roebling*, 1896. Oil on canvas, 89 x 47½ in. (226.1 x 120.7 cm). Brooklyn Museum. 1994.69.1. Gift of Paul Roebling

British

Dress, 1894

Black silk twill, taffeta, faille, and crinkled crepe; white crystal-pleated georgette; black cord embroidery; black machine-embroidered net, scrolling vine and feather motifs; black moiré ribbon
Brooklyn Museum Costume Collection at The Metropolitan Museum of Art, Gift of the Brooklyn Museum, 2009; Gift of C. W. Howard, 1950 (2009.300.1157a, b)

Queen Victoria (1819–1901) wore mourning black for thirty-three years after the death of her husband, Prince Albert, in 1861. Pleated organdy at the cuffs and neckline provide the customary touches of white that indicate a mourning stage beyond the all-black of deep mourning. This dress has exceptional status because the queen wore it in a photograph of four generations of the royal family taken at the christening of her great-grandson, Prince Edward Albert of York, who was born in June 1894. The dress is of a lightweight summer material. As even a queen has practical needs, the bodice has slit pockets at either side, while the skirt is equipped with a large patch pocket and another side pocket.

A collector and friend of the donor's father purchased the dress in 1897 at a sale of the queen's garments; Victoria discreetly held such sales annually.

W. and D. Downey (British, founded ca. 1855). *Four Generations,* from left to right: Prince Albert Edward of Wales (later King Edward VII), Prince Edward Albert of York (later King Edward VIII), Queen Victoria, and the Duke of York (later King George V), 1894. Getty Images/ Hulton Archive

Maullé
(Russian)

Dress Shirt, ca. 1900

White plain weave linen; label: "Maullé/Perspective de Nevsky 26/St. Petersbourg"
Brooklyn Museum Costume Collection at The Metropolitan Museum of Art, Gift of
the Brooklyn Museum, 2009; Gift of Alastair Bradley Martin, 1977 (2009.300.2186)

Donated to the collection in a presentation box from À La Vieille Russie, a
New York City purveyor of fine historic Russian objects, with the provenance
of having belonged to Czar Nicholas II, the shirt displays the extremely
fine workmanship and superb quality of linen that speak of royal ownership. Discreetly placed under the front button tab are the red Maullé label
with double-headed Russian imperial eagle and, below it, white embroidery
depicting the imperial cipher surmounted by a crown. Maullé provided
multiple personal services to the czar. The firm not only supplied wardrobe
necessities, such as shirts, socks, and ties, but also tended to his mending,
laundering, and barbering needs.

Franklin Simon & Company

(American, founded 1902)

Women's Motor Corps of America Uniform, 1916–18

Army green wool gabardine; light olive green plain weave cotton; brown and green tubular knit; khaki tan plain weave cotton; brown calfskin; labels: "Custom Made/Franklin Simon & Co./Fifth Avenue, N.Y." Brooklyn Museum Costume Collection at The Metropolitan Museum of Art, Gift of the Brooklyn Museum, 2009; Gift of Mrs. C. O. Stumpf, 1949 (2009.300.1155a–l)

World War I was the first war in which significant numbers of American women participated and the first in which they performed duties other than medical. The Women's Motor Corps of America was one group that was available to them. Taking advantage of the advent of the automobile, members volunteered as drivers to provide transport services at home and abroad. Their uniforms were important signifiers of the patriotic roles they were playing. This ensemble, with its Sam Brown belt and leather leggings, is similar in style to U.S. Army uniforms. Far from standard issue, however, this one was custom made at the upscale New York department store Franklin Simon & Company.

Probably American

Utility Coordinates, 1941

Blue cotton bird cloth; red velveteen; silver zippers with ring pulls
Brooklyn Museum Costume Collection at The Metropolitan Museum of Art, Gift of the Brooklyn Museum, 2009; Gift of Martha Schaeffer, 1941 (2009.300.6a–e)

Sporting eleven zippers, including two at the shoulder pouches and two on the pants legs, this three-piece utility suit was made for action and versatility. The bodice, skirt, and pants are each fitted with a zipper at the waist for a speedy change from one piece to the other. Utility coveralls were worn by women working in factories during World War II. This example, more fashionable than those, yet seemingly task-specific, was donated through the department store Abraham & Straus in 1941, before America entered the war. Its donation at that time suggests it was considered innovative. To add to its unique character, the records indicate the trade name (maker) was "Mademoiselle Mode," an unexpectedly fashionable French association for a utilitarian, and presumably American, garment.

The Brooklyn Museum collection includes broad holdings of European regional, or folk, costumes, an indigenous style of clothing that developed in the eighteenth century among the rural classes working in agricultural and other jobs related to the land. Developing as a way for groups of people connected by geography or ethnicity to distinguish themselves from each other, folk costume took many decorative and structural forms. The headwear here illustrates some of the distinctive shapes that served to identify regional groups.

French (Touraine)

Cap, 1760–90

Cotton, linen
Brooklyn Museum Costume Collection at The
Metropolitan Museum of Art, Gift of the Brooklyn
Museum, 2009; Brooklyn Museum Collection
(2009.300.2261)

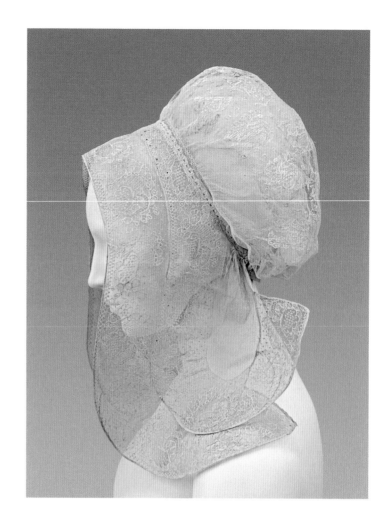

French

Cap, fourth quarter 19th century

Cream cotton organdy, bobbin lace edging; cream muslin
Brooklyn Museum Costume Collection at The
Metropolitan Museum of Art, Gift of the Brooklyn
Museum, 2009; Gift of Dorothea and Margaret Reimer,
1924 (2009.300.1677)

A decorative cap would have been worn over the
plain muslin at back.

Dutch (Friesland)

Ear Iron, fourth quarter 19th century

Brass
Brooklyn Museum Costume Collection at The
Metropolitan Museum of Art, Gift of the Brooklyn
Museum, 2009; Brooklyn Museum Collection
(2009.300.2255)

One of the most distinctive aspects of Friesian
headwear is the ear iron, a band of metal fitting
around the back of the head with ornaments at
the temples. The shape and style of the ornaments
indicated a personal attribute, such as a husband's
or son's profession, locality, or religion.

Dutch (Friesland)

Cap, second half 19th century
(worn with ear iron above)

Blue cotton net; cream machine-made lace, foliate motif
Brooklyn Museum Costume Collection at The
Metropolitan Museum of Art, Gift of the Brooklyn
Museum, 2009; Gift of Mrs. Tunis G. Bergen, 1929
(2009.300.1690a, b)

Dutch (Volendam)

Cap (Hul), first half 20th century

Cotton
Brooklyn Museum Costume Collection at The
Metropolitan Museum of Art, Gift of the Brooklyn
Museum, 2009; Gift of Sally Victor, 1949
(2009.300.1830)

The objects illustrated on these and the following four pages are part of a large collection of Russian costumes and textiles formed by Natalia de Shabelsky (1841–1905), a Russian noblewoman who was inspired to preserve what she perceived as the vanishing folk-art traditions of her native country.

Traveling extensively throughout Great Russia from the 1870s until the end of the century, she collected many fine examples of textile art, which included extravagant festive costumes worn by women from the land-owning peasant class. While the materials used were not equivalent in value to those found in the magnificent costumes worn in royal and aristocratic circles, they represent the Russian sense of opulence rendered with creativity by the hands of prosperous yet common people. Much of the collection was brought to the United States in the 1930s to be sold on behalf of the Shabelsky family. The donor purchased a large portion of it as a gift for the Brooklyn Museum.

Russian (Vladimir)

Festive Costume, 19th century

Dress (*sarafan*): blue silk damask, gold metal fringe; printed cotton lining. Blouse: peach figured weave silk; gold metallic bobbin lace; lime green damask. Bodice (*epanechka*): cream satin brocaded with polychrome floral motifs; silver foil and filé braid. Belt: brown, green, black, and white cotton
Brooklyn Museum Costume Collection at The Metropolitan Museum of Art, Gift of the Brooklyn Museum, 2009; Gift of Mrs. Edward S. Harkness in memory of her mother, Elizabeth Greenman Stillman, 1931 (2009.300.2323a–d)

Russian (Vladimir)

Headdress (Kokochnik) and Forehead Panel (Venchik), first half 19th century

Headdress: pale blue plain weave silk; silver and gold filé padded and couched embroidery; gold braid; pink and silver foil. Forehead panel: silk brocatelle, mother-of-pearl beads; glass; gold foil; stamped in Russian: "Ancient Russian Collection/Kn.V.P. Sidamon/Eristoff/Shabelsky"
Brooklyn Museum Costume Collection at The Metropolitan Museum of Art, Gift of the Brooklyn Museum, 2009; Gift of Mrs. Edward S. Harkness in memory of her mother, Elizabeth Greenman Stillman, 1931 (2009.300.1102; 2009.300.1101)

This kind of elaborate ensemble was worn to celebrate important religious holidays or personal events such as weddings. The exuberant mix of colors and patterns

typifies Russian high style. Traditional costume sometimes has its roots in forms of dress from earlier centuries. The long sleeves of the blouse are possible vestiges of the *houppelande*, a robe with long sleeves worn in fifteenth- and sixteenth-century Europe. Trailing on the ground like a train, the sleeves add to the aura of grandeur.

Russian (Vladimir)

Doll, second half 18th century

Silk; metallic; glass; pearls; linen; cotton; wood
Brooklyn Museum Costume Collection at The Metropolitan Museum of Art, Gift of the Brooklyn Museum, 2009; Gift of Mrs. Edward S. Harkness in memory of her mother, Elizabeth Greenman Stillman, 1931 (2009.300.1719)

Russian (Moscow)

Doll, second half 18th century

Silk; linen; metallic; pearls; metal; cotton; wood
Brooklyn Museum Costume Collection at The Metropolitan Museum of Art, Gift of the Brooklyn Museum, 2009; Gift of Mrs. Edward S. Harkness in memory of her mother, Elizabeth Greenman Stillman, 1931 (2009.300.1718)

Russian

Wedding Veil, first half 19th century

Red, green, yellow, and white silk ikat with metallic thread
patterning
Brooklyn Museum Costume Collection at The Metropolitan
Museum of Art, Gift of the Brooklyn Museum, 2009; Gift of
Mrs. Edward S. Harkness in memory of her mother, Elizabeth
Greenman Stillman, 1931 (2009.300.1710)

This wedding veil is woven using the ikat process, in
which the warp yarns are dyed in a pattern before weaving, producing a characteristic blurred edge. The process
is common to many cultures, but some of the most
spectacular examples are from Uzbekistan, a region formerly part of the Russian Empire. The gold metallic
threads that create medallion- and winding-lace ribbon
patterns, as well as double-headed imperial eagles at each
corner (below), add another layer of complexity to the
sophisticated design. The obvious expense and imperial
iconography suggest that the bride was from a prominent
and prosperous family.

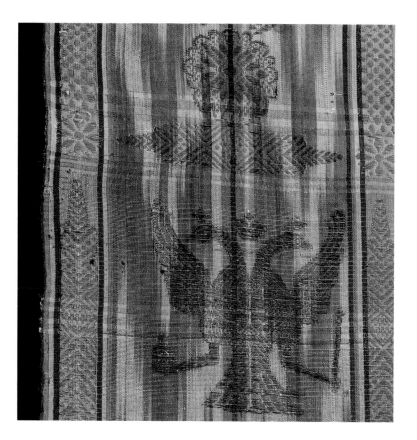

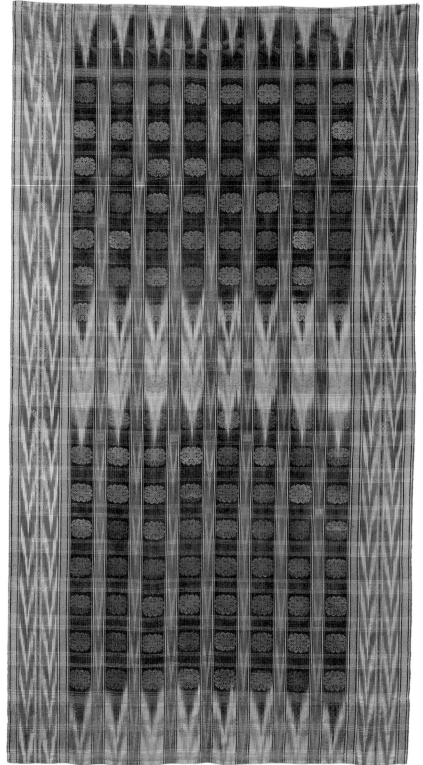

Embroidered with gold threads and decorated with colored foil, stones, freshwater pearls, and shell, the headdresses (kokochniks) were the most ornate components of festive dress. The type of decorative elements used reflected the region's natural resources. Those collected by Mme de Shabelsky were mostly from regions where river pearls were in abundance.

Russian (Olonets, Karelskaya)

Headdress, first half 19th century

Gold strip embroidery; shell beads; freshwater pearls; white cotton cord; red velvet
Brooklyn Museum Costume Collection at The Metropolitan Museum of Art, Gift of the Brooklyn Museum, 2009; Gift of Mrs. Edward S. Harkness in memory of her mother, Elizabeth Greenman Stillman, 1931 (2009.300.1105)

Russian (Kostroma)

Headdress and Forehead Panel, fourth quarter 18th century–first half 19th century

Headdress: gold metallic braid; silver purl; shell beads; freshwater pearls; cream silk; colored glass; colored foil; silk brocade, rose pattern at edges; cardboard. Forehead panel: blue silk damask; shell beads; freshwater pearls; colored glass; colored foil
Brooklyn Museum Costume Collection at The Metropolitan Museum of Art, Gift of the Brooklyn Museum, 2009; Gift of Mrs. Edward S. Harkness in memory of her mother, Elizabeth Greenman Stillman, 1931 (2009.300.1103 and 2009.300.1107)

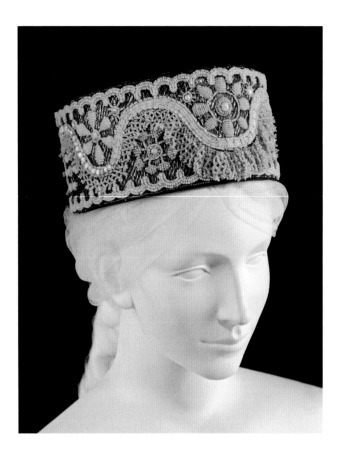

Peasant costume from Olonets. Holme, Charles, ed. *Peasant Art in Russia*. London: 'The Studio' Ltd., 1912, plate 23. Thomas J. Watson Library, The Metropolitan Museum of Art. The women in these photographs are wearing the hats illustrated here.

Peasant costume from Kostroma. Holme, Charles, ed. *Peasant Art in Russia*. London: 'The Studio' Ltd., 1912, plate 7. Thomas J. Watson Library, The Metropolitan Museum of Art. These photographs were presumably part of the Shabelsky collection. Natalia Shabelsky's daughters, Princess Alexandre Sidamon-Eristoff and Natalie Shabelsky, provided the images to the book's editor in 1912.

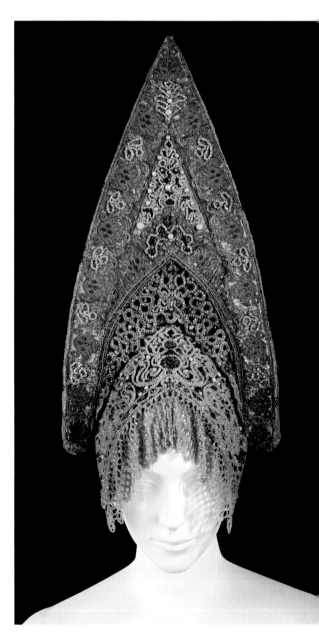

Russian (Tula)

Headdress, 19th century

Burgundy silk velvet; gold metallic lace; gold metal braid; shell beads; freshwater pearls; colored glass stones; stamped in Russian: "Ancient Russian Collection/ Kh.V.P. Sidamon/Eristoff/Shabelsky" Brooklyn Museum Costume Collection at The Metropolitan Museum of Art, Gift of the Brooklyn Museum, 2009; Gift of Mrs. Edward S. Harkness in memory of her mother, Elizabeth Greenman Stillman, 1931 (2009.300.1104)

Russian (Kaluga)

Bridal Headdress, 1790–1810

Burgundy silk velvet; gold and silver filé embroidery; sequins; gilt purl; colored metal paillettes; freshwater pearls; shell beads; cream cotton cord with bead embroidery; glass; stamped in Russian: "Ancient Russian Collection/Kn.V.P. Sidamon/ Eristoff/Shabelsky"
Brooklyn Museum Costume Collection at The Metropolitan Museum of Art, Gift of the Brooklyn Museum, 2009; Gift of Mrs. Edward S. Harkness in memory of her mother, Elizabeth Greenman Stillman, 1931 (2009.300.1106)

Initials at the sides of the crown and goddess imagery, at the center, symbolizing fertility, identify this as a bridal headdress. The fine pearl or shell bead forehead ruffle has the suppleness of fabric. The piece was collected in Kaluga Province on the Oka River, where freshwater pearls were abundant.

American

Hat, 1940–45

Olive green velvet; gold upholstery cord trim; gold painted rooster-foot ornament; label: "John Frederics, Inc./New York"; label: "Made in America/22"
Brooklyn Museum Costume Collection at The Metropolitan Museum of Art, Gift of the Brooklyn Museum, 2009; Gift of Mrs. R. A. Bernatschke, 1955 (2009.300.1242)

John P. John, one of America's top milliners, designed the original version of this hat for Vivien Leigh's character Scarlett O'Hara in the 1939 film *Gone with the Wind*. Desperate to make herself attractive, Scarlett fabricates a gown and hat decorated with rooster feet from the curtains at "Tara," her family's estate, in preparation for a visit from her suitor Rhett Butler. Scarlett's making do with what was available during wartime resonated with American society in the 1940s, when, to compensate for wartime shortages, offbeat materials were routinely appropriated for fashionable accessories. Commercial replicas such as this one were subsequently reproduced by a hat wholesaler who negotiated the rights to reproduce *Gone with the Wind* hat styles under the name John Frederics, Inc.

Vivien Leigh and Clark Gable in *Gone with the Wind* (directed by Victor Fleming), 1939. Costumes by Walter Plunkett (American, 1902–1982). MGM/ Everett

Travis Banton
(American, 1894–1958)

Evening Dress, 1934

Black silk charmeuse with gold and silver sequin embroidery
Brooklyn Museum Costume Collection at The Metropolitan Museum of Art, Gift of
the Brooklyn Museum, 2009; Gift of Anna May Wong, 1956 (2009.300.1507)

An evocative and glamorous example of the work of Paramount Studios costume designer Travis Banton, this dress was worn by Chinese-American actress Anna May Wong in her role as Tu Tuan, a nightclub entertainer in the 1934 film *Limehouse Blues*. It is an amalgam of the cheongsam, a form-fitting Chinese dress style with a narrow band collar and side front closure, and the form-fitting Western gowns of the early twentieth-century Belle Époque period that featured high band collars and sweeping trains. At the same time, it embodies 1930s glamour. The dragon motif, here executed on the front and back in dazzling overlapping gold and silver sequins, has preeminent status in the Chinese design vocabulary. Wong was a pioneer for Asian-American actors and one of the few to transition from silent to talking films.

Ray Jones (American, 1900–1975). Anna May Wong in *Limehouse Blues* (directed by Alexander Hall), 1934. Costumes by Travis Banton (American, 1894–1958). Paramount Pictures/The Kobal Collection

Sorelle Fontana

(Italian, active 1943–92), by Micol Fontana (Italian, b. 1913)

Evening Ensemble, 1954

Pink duchesse silk satin embroidered with pearlescent and iridescent sequins, beads, and black velvet appliqué
Brooklyn Museum Costume Collection at The Metropolitan Museum of Art, Gift of the Brooklyn Museum, 2009; Gift of Micol Fontana, 1954 (2009.300.1196a–d)

The Fontana sisters excelled at producing extravagant evening wear for high-profile society women and celebrities, especially film stars. In their heyday, the 1950s, their work epitomized the decade's aesthetic for wasp-waisted bouffant gowns fashioned in luxurious fabrics. Dramatic and opulent surface decoration befitting star status was a trademark. This dress was designed for the actress Ava Gardner, their most celebrated client, to wear in the 1954 film *The Barefoot Contessa*, in which she plays a woman of humble origins who becomes a movie star and then a countess. It figures prominently in a scene set in the dining room of a casino on the French

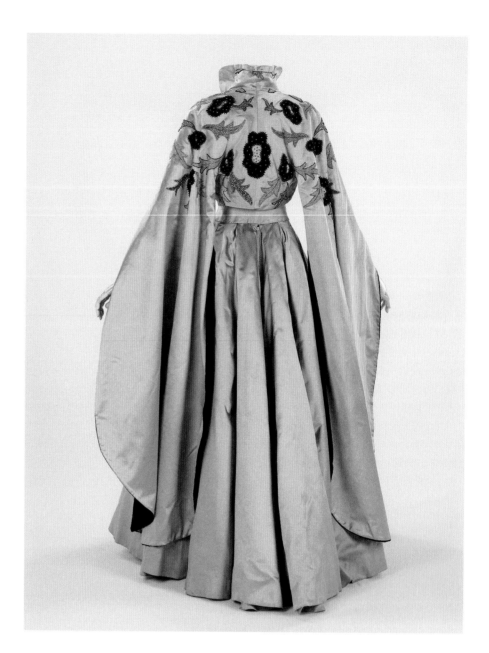

Ava Gardner in *The Barefoot Contessa* (directed by Joseph L. Mankiewicz), 1954. Costumes by Sorelle Fontana (Italian, active 1943–92). United Artists/Courtesy of Gary and Juan Carlos, www.doctormacro1.info

Riviera. Bedecked in dazzling diamond necklace and earrings, Gardner, as the movie star, sweeps into the room wearing the dress with its swinging-sleeved bolero wrap, sits down, and removes it to reveal her handsome shoulders and the décolletage of the strapless bodice. When she leaves the table, the wrap stays on the chair, marking her place. Upon her return, she covers herself once again with the wrap, as an expression of self-protection during an argument. The round stand-up collar frames her face in a close-up. Her subsequent triumphant exit on the count's arm is enhanced by the sweep of the floor-length sleeves and the glitter and contrast of the embroidery across her back.

These two garments were part of a promotional project entitled "Seven Years of Prophesy Fashions, 1963–1970." It was associated with the 1964 film "Seven Days in May," a political intrigue set in 1970. Publicist Eleanor Lambert was commissioned by the film's producer to recruit seven designers from seven countries to create their visions of 1970s styles. Fashion illustrator Joe Eula sketched each completed design.

The fashions were held at the Brooklyn Museum in an unopened trunk labeled "Time Capsule" until May 1, 1970. If there was an official opening, no documentation recording it has been found.

John Cavanagh

(British, 1914–2004)

"Basic" Jumpsuit, 1963

Cream nylon jersey; label: "John Cavanagh/London/Made in England" Brooklyn Museum Costume Collection at The Metropolitan Museum of Art, Gift of the Brooklyn Museum, 2009; Gift of Seven Arts Production, Joel Productions and Paramount Pictures Corporation, 1964 (2009.300.345)

Anticipating the comfort and practicality of bifurcated garments that would nearly obliterate the wearing of skirts in the 1970s, Cavanagh merged Greek drapery with knee-length bloomers into a one-piece futuristic design, which, according to accompanying documents, he believed would be "automatic for work, travel and all active life."

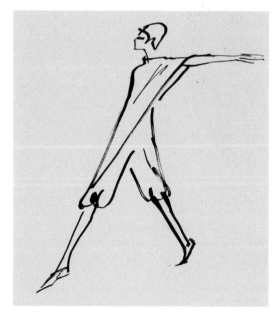

Joe Eula (American, 1925–2004). Sketch reproduction, "Basic" jumpsuit by John Cavanagh, 1963. Brooklyn Museum Costume Collection at The Metropolitan Museum of Art, Gift of the Brooklyn Museum, 2009; Courtesy of the Irene Lewisohn Costume Reference Library

Simonetta Colonna di Cesaro
(Italian, b. 1922)

Alberto Fabiani
(Italian, b. 1910)

"The 1970 Look" Ensemble, 1963

Red wool tweed; red leather buttons; red ribbed
cotton knit stocking boots, kidskin heels; label:
"Simonetta et Fabiani/Made in France"
Brooklyn Museum Costume Collection at The
Metropolitan Museum of Art, Gift of the Brooklyn
Museum, 2009; Gift of Seven Arts Productions, Joel
Productions and Paramount Pictures Corporation
(2009.300.344a–e)

Italian designers Simonetta and Fabiani
worked together in Paris under a joint
label from 1962 to 1965. Predicting that
skirts would be worn five inches above the
knee, they anticipated the style for short
skirts accompanied by compensatory
thigh-high stocking boots that took hold
at the end of the 1960s. Although it is
a promotional piece, the ensemble is of
couture quality.

Joe Eula (American, 1925–2004). Sketch reproduction, "The
1970 Look" ensemble by Simonetta et Fabiani, 1963. Brooklyn
Museum Costume Collection at The Metropolitan Museum
of Art, Gift of the Brooklyn Museum, 2009; Courtesy of the
Irene Lewisohn Costume Reference Library

In 1947 an American grassroots campaign sent a large-scale relief package containing food and other supplies to France in response to the hardships its citizens endured during World War II. Shipped in boxcars, it was dubbed the "American Friendship Train." The following year the people of France, moved by this generosity, organized a gift in kind. The "Gratitude," or "Merci," Train was a set of forty-nine boxcars filled with gifts of thanks that ranged from handmade children's toys to works of art. Each of the forty-eight states was to receive a boxcar. The forty-ninth was to be shared between Washington, D.C., and the Territory of Hawaii.

For its contribution, the Chambre Syndicale de la Couture Parisienne, governing body of the French couture industry, opted to create a set of fashion mannequins like the ones they had produced in 1947 for a promotional display entitled "Théâtre de la Mode." The theme for the project was the evolution of 200 years of French fashion. Each couturier chose a year between 1715 and 1906 from which to interpret a costume. Their sources included works of art, literature, and historic fashion plates.

The couture houses lavished upon these miniature emissaries of good will the same level of skill, care, and attention to detail that they applied to their full-sized counterparts. The unique open-wire construction of the bodies, which measured twenty-four inches high, provided the flexibility required to replicate each period's fashionable posture, while individualized faces could be molded from the plaster heads. Top hairstylists fashioned the human-hair period coiffures, and preeminent accessories designers supplied the items necessary for a complete ensemble. The mannequin bodies were designed by the French illustrator Eliane Bonabel (b. 1920) and the heads by the Spanish sculptor Joan Rebull (1899–1981).

The original intention was to include one doll in each boxcar; but recognizing the Brooklyn Museum's reputation as the country's most prominent center for the study of fashion design, the Chambre Syndicale chose the newly opened Design Lab at the museum as the repository for them all.

Soon after the dolls were accessioned, the museum published a booklet from which the caption information provided here was taken.[2]

Jean-Michel Moreau le Jeune (French, 1741–1814). *Les Adieux*, engraved by Robert Delaunay (French, 1749–1814), from *Le Monument du costume*, 1777. Etching and engraving. The Metropolitan Museum of Art, Harris Brisbane Dick Fund, 1934 (34.22.1)

Jean Dessès
(French, born Egypt, 1904–1970)

"1774 Doll," 1949

Hat designer: Gervais
Metal; plaster; hair; silk; feather; leather; metallic; glass; cotton; artificial flowers; label: "Jean Dessès/17.Avenue Matignon.Paris"
Brooklyn Museum Costume Collection at The Metropolitan Museum of Art, Gift of the Brooklyn Museum, 2009; Gift of Chambre Syndicale de la Couture Parisienne, 1949 (2009.300.701)

Les Adieux by Jean-Michel Moreau le Jeune provided the inspiration for this dress. Moreau le Jeune (1741–1814) was a French illustrator and engraver best known for his images recording fashionable dress and interiors.

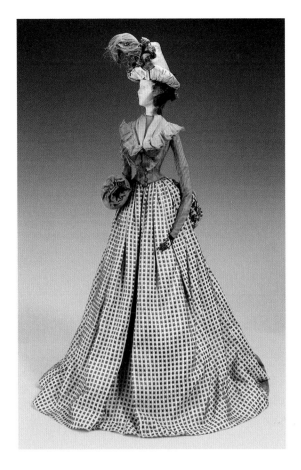  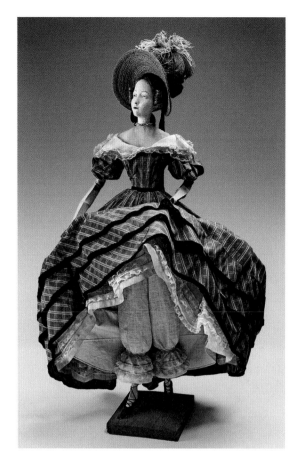

Martial & Armand
(French)

"1791 Doll," 1949

Other designers: hat, Evelyne Arzan (French); hair, Henri Durand (French)
Metal; plaster; hair; silk; feather; artificial flowers; label: "Martial & Armand, place Vendome Paris"
Brooklyn Museum Costume Collection at The Metropolitan Museum of Art, Gift of the Brooklyn Museum, 2009; Gift of Chambre Syndicale de la Couture Parisienne, 1949 (2009.300.714)

An unidentified engraving by Léopold Boilly (1761–1845), the French genre painter and engraver, was the inspiration for this design.

Jeanne Lafaurie
(French)

"1797 Doll," 1949

Other designers: hat, Jean Barthet (French); shoes, Garabedian (French); hair, Marcel Maggy (French)
Metal; plaster; hair; wool; silk; feather
Brooklyn Museum Costume Collection at The Metropolitan Museum of Art, Gift of the Brooklyn Museum, 2009; Gift of Chambre Syndicale de la Couture Parisienne, 1949 (2009.300.700)

Marcelle Dormoy
(French)

"1832 Doll," 1949

Other designers: hat, Rose Descat (French); hair, Antoine (French)
Metal; plaster; hair; silk; straw; cotton; feather; linen
Brooklyn Museum Costume Collection at The Metropolitan Museum of Art, Gift of the Brooklyn Museum, 2009; Gift of Chambre Syndicale de la Couture Parisienne, 1949 (2009.300.711)

Dormoy's creation was designed after a dress by the couturière Mlle Palmyre, whose salon served the French ruling class, including Queen Marie-Amélie and later Empress Eugénie. The dress is from the reign of King Louis-Philippe (1830–48), to whom Marie-Amélie was consort.

Madeleine de Rauch
(French)

"1830 Doll," 1949

Other designers: hat, Claude (French); gloves, Roger Faré
(French)
Metal; plaster; hair; wool; silk; straw; leather
Brooklyn Museum Costume Collection at The Metropolitan
Museum of Art, Gift of the Brooklyn Museum, 2009;
Gift of Chambre Syndicale de la Couture Parisienne, 1949
(2009.300.719)

This riding habit is one of two in the group that
represent sporting apparel.

Marcelle Chaumont
(French, 1891–1990)

"1866 Doll," 1949

Other designers: hat, Caroline Reboux (French, 1835–1927)
hair, Georgel
Metal; plaster; hair; silk; label: "M. Chaumont/19. Avenue
George V Paris"
Brooklyn Museum Costume Collection at The Metropolitan
Museum of Art, Gift of the Brooklyn Museum, 2009;
Gift of Chambre Syndicale de la Couture Parisienne, 1949
(2009.300.722)

An unidentified painting by the German artist
Franz Xaver Winterhalter (1805–1873) was
Chaumont's inspiration for this ensemble.

Pierre Balmain
(French, 1914–1982)

"1888 Doll," 1949

Hair designer: Albert Pourière
Metal; plaster; hair; wool; fur; leather; feather; wood; silk;
sequins
Brooklyn Museum Costume Collection at The Metropolitan
Museum of Art, Gift of the Brooklyn Museum, 2009;
Gift of Chambre Syndicale de la Couture Parisienne, 1949
(2009.300.720)

The inspiration for this ensemble was a design
created by Charles Frederick Worth for Empress
Elizabeth of Austria (1837–1898), wife of Emperor
Franz Joseph (1830–1916), known for her keen
sense of fashion and beauty.

Calixte
(French)

"1900 Doll," 1949

Other designers: hat, Maud et Nano (French); hair, Phyris
(French)
Metal; plaster; hair; silk; cotton; rhinestones
Brooklyn Museum Costume Collection at The Metropolitan
Museum of Art, Gift of the Brooklyn Museum, 2009;
Gift of Chambre Syndicale de la Couture Parisienne, 1949
(2009.300.726a, b)

Robert Piguet
(French, born Switzerland, 1901–1953)

"1902 Doll," 1949

Other designers: hat, Paulette (French); parasol, Vedrenne
(French); hair, Fernand Aubry (French)
Metal; plaster; hair; silk; straw; cotton; feather; wood;
label: "Vedrenne/rue St. Roch/Paris"
Brooklyn Museum Costume Collection at The Metropolitan
Museum of Art, Gift of the Brooklyn Museum, 2009;
Gift of Chambre Syndicale de la Couture Parisienne, 1949
(2009.300.727)

Elsa Schiaparelli
(French, born Italy, 1890–1973)

"1906 Doll," 1949

Other designers: boots, Perugia (French, founded 1909);
hair, Antoine (French)
Metal; plaster; hair; wool; silk; leather; rhinestones;
imitation pearls; feather; label: "Schiaparelli/Paris"
Brooklyn Museum Costume Collection at The Metropolitan
Museum of Art, Gift of the Brooklyn Museum, 2009;
Gift of Chambre Syndicale de la Couture Parisienne, 1949
(2009.1445a–d)

Shoes 1600s–1970s

Shoes can be said to be the most fascinating and essential of fashion accessories. Although stylish hats, bags and gloves are decorative and most often functional, they can be replaced or omitted. Shoes, however, must support the mobile human body and protect the bottom of the foot. At the same time, they are important expressions of style; objects of beauty, chic, and whimsy. Their creative possibilities are limited only by the shape and mechanics of the foot, around which they are sculpted and to which they must adhere. In this duality of purpose, innovative technology and aesthetics play equal roles. Experimentation with materials is primary to carrying out both. In the brief sampling on the following pages is a wide range: silks that are plain or have woven designs; textured leathers in solid colors or stamped with patterns; kidskin with gleaming metalized, pearlized, and painted surfaces; fabrics embroidered with wool, metallic threads, and silk chenille; cotton lace formed into bootees; transparent vinyl; nylon thread sewn through soles to form uppers; and metal cast into a decorative heels.

The shoes were selected to give a broad overview of three centuries of the technology and design of footwear. Even in this brief survey, some trends, among them changes in heel heights and degree of foot exposure, are evident. Heels plummeted from three and even four inches at the end of the eighteenth century to vestigial proportions and then became flat, remaining so until 1850, when a low chunky version was introduced. This heel became the norm, with slight variations, until the 1890s, when there was a precipitous spike upward. The lower heel was reinstated at the turn of the century and remained the mode until the 1920s, when heights of three inches, or sometimes more, were worn for evening. Fluctuations in heights followed, gradually climbing upward, particularly in evening styles. The ascendance culminated in the four-inch-plus slender spike of the late 1950s. Although the four-inch heel is a sufficient challenge for most, greater heights have since been designed and worn in extreme displays of fashion's artifice.

Foot exposure took a giant step backward in the seventeenth century, after open-toed, backless chopines were replaced by high heels with closed toes and backs. With the exception of the mule, mainstream shoes did not expose the heel or toe again until the late 1930s, when open-toed and sling-back styles gained acceptance.

Brooklyn owes its extensive footwear holdings, which date from the seventeenth century to the 1990s, to the donations of countless individuals; shoes were often included, and sometimes outnumbered, the clothing in gifts of personal wardrobes. However, there are four donations exclusively of footwear that make up the collection's core and establish its unique character.

The first was a gift, in 1947, from Steven Arpad of shoe prototypes accompanied by an extensive drawings archive he created in Paris in 1939. During that decade Arpad worked as the exclusive shoe designer for French couturier Balenciaga and as an independent for Delman and I. Miller, while simultaneously operating an embroidery and jewelry business. He moved to New York in 1940 and there continued his multifaceted career, which included providing jeweled embroidery for American designers such as Norman Norell, Pauline Trigere, and Beth Levine.

In 1954 and 1955, Herman Delman, founder and owner of the upscale company that still bears his name, made a gift of more than 150 items of historic footwear. Nearly all are from the eighteenth and nineteenth centuries; some are especially rare. The museum's unique group of high-fashion footwear from the mid-1950s was acquired in 1960 when Charline Osgood, Director of the Kid Leather Guild, donated some 170 European examples, mostly Italian, by preeminent makers such as Alberto Dal Cò, Mario Valentino, and Albanese. Finally, holdings of American footwear from the late 1940s to the early 1970s were artistically and numerically enhanced in 1994, when designer Beth Levine made a donation of some sixty items that includes signature examples of her innovative and witty output and represents more than twenty-five years of her career.

Opposite: André Perugia, *Evening Sandal* (back), 1928–29

Venetian

Chopines, 1550–1650

Green silk velvet; light green taffeta
ribbon; gold metallic lace and braid
Brooklyn Museum Costume Collection at
The Metropolitan Museum of Art, Gift of
the Brooklyn Museum, 2009; Gift of
Herman Delman (2009.300.1494a, b)

Originating as an upper-class fashion in fifteenth-century Venice,
these high clogs designated the ele-
vated social status of the wearer.
The style gradually became associated with prostitutes, and by the
early seventeenth century the upper
classes stopped wearing them and
donned high heels.

British

Shoes, 1750–69

White, blue, red, yellow, and green wool,
needlepoint flame-stitch design on linen
ground; cream silk plain weave with black,
pale green, and pink printed foliate design
Brooklyn Museum Costume Collection at
The Metropolitan Museum of Art, Gift of
the Brooklyn Museum, 2009; Gift of Mrs.
Clarence R. Hyde, 1928 (2009.300.1407a, b)

This latchet shoe, the classic style
of women's footwear for most of
the eighteenth century, was worn
with a large decorative buckle that
secured the two tabs (latchets)
across the top of the foot. The flame-
stitch pattern of the canvaswork
embroidery used for the uppers is
commonly seen in eighteenth-
century furnishings and small fashion accessories. It may have been
worked at home to be made into
shoes. Impractical for footwear, the
printed-silk heel covering is rare.

British

Shoes, 1732–59

Burgundy and cream voided ciselé silk velvet, floral vine pattern on striped ground; patterned gold metallic tape; red kidskin
Brooklyn Museum Costume Collection at The Metropolitan Museum of Art, Gift of the Brooklyn Museum, 2009; Gift of Mrs. Clarence R. Hyde, 1928 (2009.300.1410a, b)

Robustly patterned fabrics such as this one were a common choice for the footwear of aristocratic women in the late seventeenth and early eighteenth centuries. The rand, a narrow strip of leather (here white) around the sole edge of the vamp, is a feature of high-quality shoes of the first half of the eighteenth century. It was phased out about 1760.

European

Boots, 1795–1810

Blue grained kidskin bound in lavender silk ribbon; black-stained wood button; steel buckle
Brooklyn Museum Costume Collection at The Metropolitan Museum of Art, Gift of the Brooklyn Museum, 2009; Gift of Herman Delman, 1954 (2009.300.1486a, b)

Boots were worn by women in the last quarter of the eighteenth century, but their use was limited primarily to the outdoors. Few pairs survive. These extremely rare examples are constructed with flaps that wrap around the leg and then taper to a narrow strap buckled at the outside front. The style was thought to provide more protection than the standard laced closure.

J. Staton
(British)

Slippers, 1795–1805

Yellow kidskin printed in alternating bands of circles and ellipses; yellow silk ribbon; label: "J. Staton/Maker/Charing Cross/Retail & for Exportation"
Brooklyn Museum Costume Collection at The Metropolitan Museum of Art, Gift of the Brooklyn Museum, 2009; Gift of Mr. and Mrs. William Sterling Peters, 1924 (2009.300.1404a, b)

As the taste for simplicity in fashion was taking hold from the 1780s on, slipper styles gradually replaced the heavier latchet shoe. A particularly fine example of stencil-printed leather, this design has an interesting optical effect of yellow mesh over a black ground. Lively patterns were counterpoints to the plain white cotton dresses of the period.

American

Shoes with pattens, 1825–30

Red grained leather
Brooklyn Museum Costume Collection at The Metropolitan Museum of Art, Gift of the Brooklyn Museum, 2009; Gift of Herman Delman, 1954 (2009.300.1488a–f)

By the 1820s, ankle boots were in favor as daytime footwear for women in both the United States and Europe, especially for taking long walks, a practice known as "pedestrianism." Since fashionable shoes and boots were made with thin soles, some, such as this pair, had matching pattens, which the shoe fits into to provide heavier soles for walking. Shoes with their original pattens are rare.

Gundry & Son
(British)

Evening Slippers, 1840–49

Cream silk satin; gold metallic braid; label: "Gundry & Son, Boot & Shoe Makers to the Queen, the Queen Dowager, Their Royal Highnesses the Duchess of Kent & Princess Sophia/1 Soho Square, London"
Brooklyn Museum Costume Collection at The Metropolitan Museum of Art, Gift of the Brooklyn Museum, 2009; Gift of Herman Delman, 1954 (2009.300.1463a, b)

Although mid-Victorian dresses were floor length, decorated vamps with ribbon stripes, as seen here, made for an elegant impression when a toe was revealed during walking or dancing. The square toe had been in fashion for ten years when this shoe was made and would remain so for the next fifty years. The well-preserved label, boasting no fewer than four royal connections, is of interest as an early advertisement, which takes advantage of the power of association with the social elite.

French

Evening Boots, 1860–69

Cream silk satin; cream tissue taffeta ribbon cockade rosette
Brooklyn Museum Costume Collection at The Metropolitan Museum of Art, Gift of the Brooklyn Museum, 2009; Gift of Mrs. G. Brinton Roberts, 1946 (2009.300.1439a–d)

When the cage crinoline replaced heavy layers of petticoats, skirts swayed back and forth, revealing more leg than was considered proper. Ankle boots provided the solution. They were worn regularly for day and were an option to slippers for evening. This pair is typical except for the especially refined curves at the top edge. Front lacing was predominant until the 1870s, when it was supplanted by button closures.

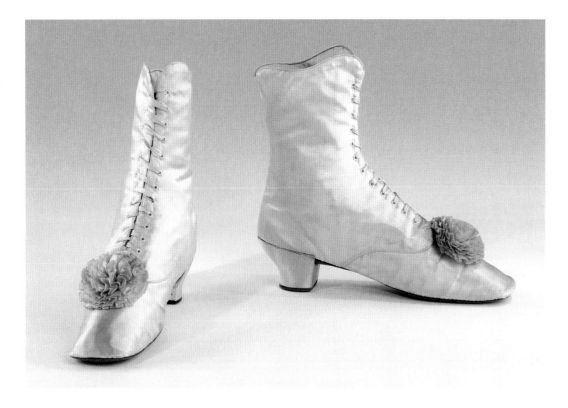

French

Evening Shoes, 1875–85

Cream silk satin; floral ribbonwork; cream, yellow, and green chenille thread embroidery; cream satin-backed grosgrain ribbon
Brooklyn Museum Costume Collection at The Metropolitan Museum of Art, Gift of the Brooklyn Museum, 2009; Gift of Mrs. Frederick H. Prince, Jr., 1967 (2009.300.1581a, b)

Embodying the finest of French craftsmanship and design, these ankle-tie evening shoes are exceptional in cut as well as in decoration. The quarters (sides) are stepped at back and have large eyelets to accommodate luxurious satin-backed grosgrain ribbon ties; the exquisite ribbonwork, more commonly applied to dresses, is the ultimate refinement for footwear.

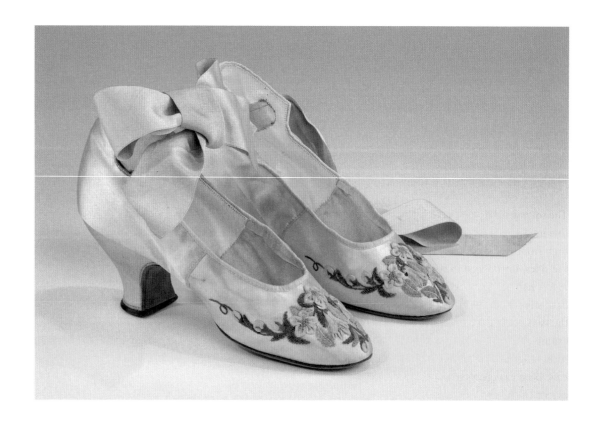

J. Ferry
(French)

Evening Slippers, 1880

Black silk satin brocaded with green, cream, pink, yellow, and blue floral and ribbon design; label: "Ferry/Paris"
Brooklyn Museum Costume Collection at The Metropolitan Museum of Art, Gift of the Brooklyn Museum, 2009; Gift of Mrs. Frederick H. Prince, Jr., 1967 (2009.300.1584a, b)

Revivals of Baroque and Rococo styles appeared in shoes starting in the 1860s. Fashioned with a replication of an eighteenth-century floral brocade, Louis heels, and latchet-like bows, these slippers are an updated version of the latchet shoe that was the style for much of the eighteenth century.

Rosenbloom's
(American)

Slippers, ca. 1892

Red grained leather; label: "Rosenbloom's/
Syracuse"
Brooklyn Museum Costume Collection at
The Metropolitan Museum of Art, Gift of
the Brooklyn Museum, 2009; Gift of
Charlene Osgood, 1965 (2009.300.1555a, b)

The so-called Juliet (or its masculine incarnation, the Romeo) with
high front and back and low V at
the sides, introduced in the early
1890s, had become one of the standard slipper cuts by the turn of
the twentieth century. This early
example in red grained leather features long curving points, which
have been exaggerated to a comical
extent.

J. Ferry
(French)

Shoes, ca. 1906

Red kidskin; satin ribbon; label: "Ferry/
Paris"
Brooklyn Museum Costume Collection at
The Metropolitan Museum of Art, Gift of
the Brooklyn Museum, 2009; Gift of Mrs.
Frederick H. Prince, Jr., 1967
(2009.300.1580a, b)

Although colorful footwear was in
vogue in the relatively flamboyant
1890s, by the turn of the century,
black, brown, and white were considered the appropriate hues for day.
Other colors were preserved for evening or special occasions. These
low-cut pumps, with mock ties at
the throat, were meticulously handmade by one of the most exclusive
shoemakers working in Paris at
the time.

Pietro Yantorny

(French, born Italy, 1874–1936)

Mules, 1914–19

Green silk damask, gilt silver strip embroidery
Brooklyn Museum Costume Collection at The
Metropolitan Museum of Art, Gift of the
Brooklyn Museum, 2009; Gift of Mercedes de
Acosta, 1953 (2009.300.1459a, b)

An interpretation of the babouche, the
traditional heelless Turkish slipper associated with the harem, this style was
especially appropriate for the Western
boudoir. It was custom made for Rita
de Acosta Lydig (see "French Couture"),
whose idiosyncratic taste in fashion
embraced an Orientalist aesthetic.
Similar to that on Turkish examples,
the embroidered fabric is probably
authentic.

Charles Strohbeck, Inc.

(American)

Evening Shoes, ca. 1920

Golden yellow, blue, and black cotton and silk,
foliate pattern
Brooklyn Museum Costume Collection at The
Metropolitan Museum of Art, Gift of the
Brooklyn Museum, 2009; Gift of Charles
Strohbeck, 1964 (2009.300.3265a, b)

Brooklyn was an important center for
fashionable shoe production in the late
nineteenth and early twentieth centuries. High-fashion shoes were known
generally in the industry as "Brooklyn
shoes." This pair of medium quality
with modish T-straps shows the extreme
toe and distorted shape of high-styled
shoes made from 1918 to 1922. The figured fabric imitating embroidery would
have been considered trendy, in contrast
to a more versatile solid.

Pietro Yantorny
(French, born Italy, 1874–1936)

Shoes, 1925–30

White suede
Brooklyn Museum Costume Collection at The
Metropolitan Museum of Art, Gift of the Brooklyn
Museum, 2009; Gift of Mrs. Edward G. Sparrow, 1969
(2009.300.2144a–d)

Lace-up shoes with "strappy" cutouts are a classic 1920s day style. Yantorny sought to create the
most perfectly crafted shoes possible for an
exclusive clientele. He invented the looped lacing
system seen on this pair in 1916 and was granted
a U.S. patent in 1920. It was intended to improve
fit and comfort, eliminate bulk, reduce wear on
the laces, and provide superior rain protection.
The elegant and distinctive curve of the inside
heel is a hallmark of Yantorny shoes.

French
Made for Marshall Field & Co. (American, founded
1881)

Evening Shoes, ca. 1927

Pearlescent fuchsia and peach kidskin; clear rhinestones;
gold metallic kidskin piping; label: "Made Expressly for
Marshall Field & Co. Paris"; label: "Modele Déposées"
Brooklyn Museum Costume Collection at The
Metropolitan Museum of Art, Gift of the Brooklyn
Museum, 2009; Gift of Herman Delman, 1955
(2009.300.1206a, b)

Shoe design gained in importance during the
1920s, when hemlines rose to knee level. As a
result, types of footwear styles and materials
multiplied exponentially. Metallic leathers and
lively appliqués were important elements in evening footwear meant to accompany the glittering flapper dresses of the 1920s. This example is
extraordinary for the flashy offbeat colors and
pearlized effect of the leather, as well as for the
gold kidskin piping meticulously applied at the
edges. Sparkling pavé rhinestones at the instep
call added attention to the wearer's beautifully
shod feet.

André Perugia

(French, 1893–1977)

Evening Sandals, 1928–29

Silver and gold metallic kidskin; cast gilt metal;
label; "Perugia/Nice/11 Faubg. St. Honoré Paris"
Brooklyn Museum Costume Collection at The
Metropolitan Museum of Art, Gift of the Brooklyn
Museum, 2009; Gift of Mrs. Carleton Putnam, 1981
(2009.300.1612a, b)

This pair of evening sandals represents the
height of progressive design and craftsmanship for which Perugia, premier French
shoemaker of his day, was known. The
extraordinary gilt-metal heel is cast in the
ornate mode of Art Deco artisans such as
Edgar Brandt, Louis Süe, and André Mare,
while the daringly bare open back was
extremely advanced, if not shocking, for
the period. An exquisite wreath-motif
metal buckle is a finishing refinement.

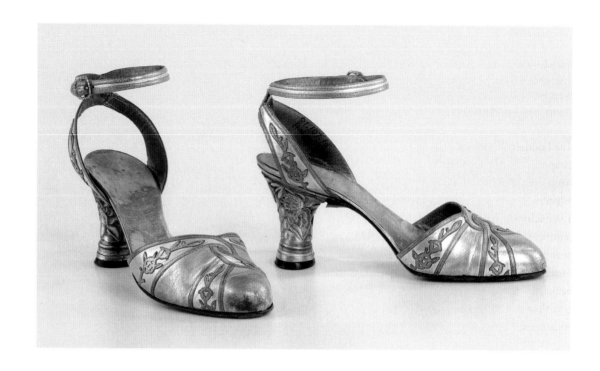

Delman, Inc.

(American, founded 1919)

Evening Shoes, 1935–40

Black silk satin; gold metallic kidskin; cream
pearlescent plastic; multicolored rhinestones; label:
"Created by Delman/New York and Paris"
Brooklyn Museum Costume Collection at The
Metropolitan Museum of Art, Gift of the Brooklyn
Museum, 2009; Gift of Herman Delman, 1955
(2009.300.1207a, b)

Herman Delman, known for his promotional savvy, was the showman of the New
York footwear industry. This tour-de-force
pair of unworn oversized T-straps may have
been made for exhibition purposes. They
feature the coat of arms of the City of Paris
with the motto "Fluctuat nec mergitur" (It
is tossed by the waves but does not sink).
The drawing style of the motto is similar to
that sometimes seen on mid-eighteenth-
century high heels.

French

Evening Slippers, 1935–49

Silver metallic leather, embossed and hand-painted in green tones
Brooklyn Museum Costume Collection at The Metropolitan Museum of Art, Gift of the Brooklyn Museum, 2009; Gift of Rodman A. Heeren, 1962 (2009.300.1295a, b)

The boudoir slipper was a standard item of apparel for the fashionable woman from the eighteenth to the early twentieth century. By the 1930s, they were an anachronism, but fantasy shoes, as represented by this pair, would have been appropriate for at-home entertaining. The hand-painted decoration and peaks at toe, throat, and heel back, give them a flavor of what was then considered Eastern exoticism.

André Perugia

(French, 1893–1977)

Boots, ca. 1939

Pale tan glazed kidskin; horn buttons; label: "Perugia/Sté Padova/2 Rue de la Paix_Paris"; "Padova/Paris"
Brooklyn Museum Costume Collection at The Metropolitan Museum of Art, Gift of the Brooklyn Museum, 2009; Gift of Millicent Huttleston Rogers, 1951 (2009.300.3136a, b)

The ankle boot was briefly revived in the years around 1939. Although not a mainstream style, it was included in the collections of numerous designers, including Elsa Schiaparelli. This elegant pair is Perugia's modern interpretation of the side-buttoned ankle boot prevalent in the 1880s. His modern twist places the buttons at side front rather than close to the ankle. Skillfully rendered crenellations appear at the top edges.

Salvatore Ferragamo

(Italian, 1898–1960)

Evening Sandals, 1938

Silver metallic kidskin; black silk satin; silver-tone metal filigree set with clear rhinestones; stamped: "Ferragamo's Creations/Florence, Italy"; stamped: "Hand Made in Italy"; "Patent Applied For" Brooklyn Museum Costume Collection at The Metropolitan Museum of Art, Gift of the Brooklyn Museum, 2009; Gift of Brooklyn Museum Fair, 1956 (2009.300.1505a, b)

Taking inspiration from the fifteenth-century chopine, master Italian shoemaker Salvatore Ferragamo pioneered the development of the wedge heel and platform sole in the 1930s. This pair is one of the most elaborately decorated of his platform styles. They were sold at Saks Fifth Avenue for one hundred dollars, an exorbitant price for a pair of sandals at the time.

Victor

(American)

Sandals, ca. 1940

Red suede
Brooklyn Museum Costume Collection at The Metropolitan Museum of Art, Gift of the Brooklyn Museum, 2009; Gift of Vivian Mook Baer in memory of Sylvia Terner Mook, 1983 (2009.300.1614a, b)

In an even more direct reference to the chopine, the designer of this shoe created an original high-style version of the platform with an undercut heel, a shape introduced by American designer Seymour Troy in 1939. Some of the most innovative examples of platforms were designed between 1938 and 1942.

Salvatore Ferragamo

(Italian, 1898–1960)

"Luito" Shoes, 1947–50

Cream kidskin; clear nylon thread; label:
"Ferragamo's Creations/Florence Italy"; "Hand
Made in Italy"
Brooklyn Museum Costume Collection at The
Metropolitan Museum of Art, Gift of the
Brooklyn Museum, 2009; Gift of Brooklyn
Museum Fair, 1956 (2009.300.1244a, b)

Semitransparent elements are notable
features of Ferragamo's mature works.
They are epitomized by his iconic
"invisible sandal" of 1947, on which the
upper is formed by a single nylon thread
passed back and forth through holes in
the sole. On this lesser-known tie version,
the thread passes through a neutral-
colored binding, retaining the most
minimal structure on the otherwise
dematerialized upper.

"Booty" Cocktail Boots, 1947

Tavernelle cotton lace; black suede; label:
"Ferragamo's Creations/Florence Italy"; "Hand
Made in Italy"
Brooklyn Museum Costume Collection at The
Metropolitan Museum of Art, Gift of the
Brooklyn Museum, 2009; Gift of the Italian
Government, 1954 (2009.300.1184a, b)

Ferragamo began using needle lace
made in the Umbrian town of
Tavernelle for shoe uppers in the late
1920s. The resulting semitransparent
effect is seen in many of the designer's
works, particularly those of the 1940s
and 1950s. Although ankle boots are
somewhat atypical of the period, the
style was favored by Ferragamo and
included in many of his collections.

Beth Levine

(American, 1913–2006) for Herbert Levine, Inc. (American, active 1946–1976)

Boots, ca. 1968

Tan kidskin; label: "Herbert Levine"; "Bonwit Teller/Fifth Ave."
Brooklyn Museum Costume Collection at The Metropolitan Museum of Art, Gift of the Brooklyn Museum, 2009; Gift of Lady Emilia Dreher Armstrong (2009.300.86.8.1a, b)

The late 1960s fashion for increasingly shorter skirts prompted the need for a thigh-high version of the fashion boot, which Levine was instrumental in revivifying earlier in the decade. Although she pioneered stretch vinyl pull-on examples of the elongated style, she included a back zipper on this fine leather alternative to achieve the glovelike fit.

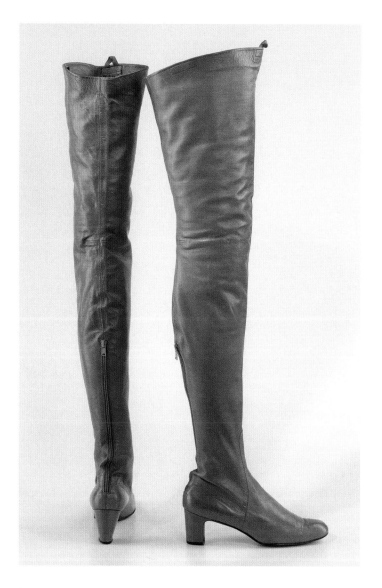

Shoes, 1953

Black silk satin; nylon fishnet mesh; leather; label: "Herbert Levine/Fine Shoes"; "Hand Lasted"
Brooklyn Museum Costume Collection at The Metropolitan Museum of Art, Gift of the Brooklyn Museum, 2009; Gift of Beth Levine in memory of her husband, Herbert, 1994 (2009.300.2240a, b)

Top American shoe designer Beth Levine was particularly adept at predicting future trends and devising structural innovations. This is the first version of her original stocking shoe design, which she repeated in various forms beginning in the mid-1950s and continuing through the late 1960s. Later examples included pantyhose tops. This style was extremely avant-garde for the early 1950s and considered risqué when it was introduced.

Between 1954 and 1959, Charline Osgood, director of the Kid Leather Guild, took annual trips to Europe, where kid leather was widely used in the making of shoes. The goal was to educate American shoe manufacturers about its benefits; in the United States at this time kid was mainly a leather for gloves. She collected more than 170 examples of footwear, produced mostly by Italy's preeminent designers and makers. Comments drawn from her presentations to the trade after each trip are included here, along with three pairs of shoes from her collection, which she donated to the Brooklyn Museum in 1960.

Mario Valentino
Italian (1927–1991)

Sandals, 1955

Burgundy suede; black patent leather; label: "Creazioni M. Valentino/Made in Italy"
Brooklyn Museum Costume Collection at The Metropolitan Museum of Art, Gift of the Brooklyn Museum, 2009; Gift of Charline Osgood, 1960 (2009.300.1270a, b)

This pair of sandals was designed with a matching pair of gloves, with the aim of promoting among American manufacturers glove–shoe coordination and the use of kid. Osgood noted that the design illustrated the trend from a wide, open toe to a closed toe and also suggested that it would be particularly appropriate for the American market in different heel heights.

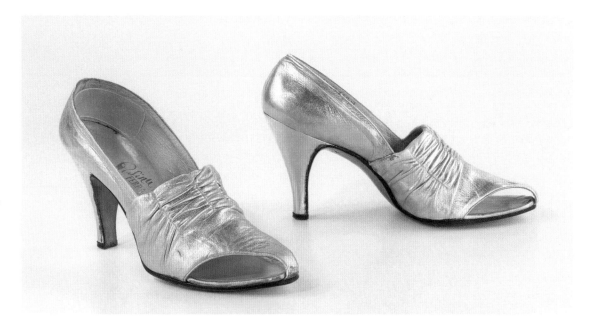

Rosina Ferragamo Schiavone
(Italian)

Evening Pumps, 1955

Gold metallic kidskin; label: "Creations Rosina Ferragamo Schiavone/Florence (Italy)"
Brooklyn Museum Costume Collection at The Metropolitan Museum of Art, Gift of the Brooklyn Museum, 2009; Gift of Charline Osgood, 1960 (2009.300.1269a, b)

The unusual cut of the vamp of these pumps, which provocatively reveals the toes on either side of their narrow closed tips, and the soft top shirring suggest the intimacy of a boudoir slipper. Osgood presented them as examples of the trend toward a closed toe and noted that the fine fit of the shoe to the heel and arch keeps it secure on the foot despite the very low quarters (sides).

Alberto Dal Cò
(Italian, 1902–1963)

Shoes, 1958

Black velvet-finished suede; gold metallic kidskin
piping and lining; label: "Dal Cò/Roma"
Brooklyn Museum Costume Collection at The
Metropolitan Museum of Art, Gift of the Brooklyn
Museum, 2009; Gift of Charline Osgood, 1960
(2009.300.1261a, b)

Although the name Alberto Dal Cò is not
well known today, the inventiveness and
superb craftsmanship evidenced in his
footwear place him in the top tier of mas-
ters of his trade. The superb line and
unique heel treatment of this elegant pair
of shoes are typical of his work. Osgood
selected them to illustrate how the silhouette draws the eye up the body of the foot
and down the back of it, a design trend
intended to create a sense of movement.
The peaked toe was a popular style in Italy
that never caught on in the United States.

Beth Levine
(American, 1913–2006) for Herbert Levine, Inc.
(American, active 1946–1976)

Evening Boots, ca. 1962

Tan and silver metallic silk, paisley pattern;
variably sized prong-set white rhinestones;
label: "Herbert Levine"
Brooklyn Museum Costume Collection at The
Metropolitan Museum of Art, Gift of the Brooklyn
Museum, 2009; Gift of Lady Emilia Dreher
Armstrong, 1989 (2009.300.2230a, b)

Levine resurrected the high-fashion boot
with designs such as this one in the early
1960s. It is a transitional style incorporating the currently fashionable stiletto heel,
while presaging the flat go-go ankle boots
André Courrèges introduced with his
"Space Age" ensembles of 1964. Heavy
metallic fabrics and dense rhinestone and
bead decorations would characterize high-
end evening wear of the decade.

242

Beth Levine

(American, 1913–2006) for Herbert Levine, Inc. (American, active 1946–1976)

Shoes, ca. 1965

Clear vinyl and cast acrylic; silver metallic kidskin; label: "Herbert Levine"
Brooklyn Museum Costume Collection at The Metropolitan Museum of Art, Gift of the Brooklyn Museum, 2009; Gift of Beth Levine in memory of her husband, Herbert, 1994 (2009.300.2239a, b)

Levine's original work with vinyl was among her acknowledged achievements. Picking up on Ferragamo's innovations in the dematerialization of form, she fashioned a nearly invisible loafer, an unexpectedly casual shoe to design in the transparent idiom. Levine patented a method for attaching clear acrylic heels without screws for complete transparency.

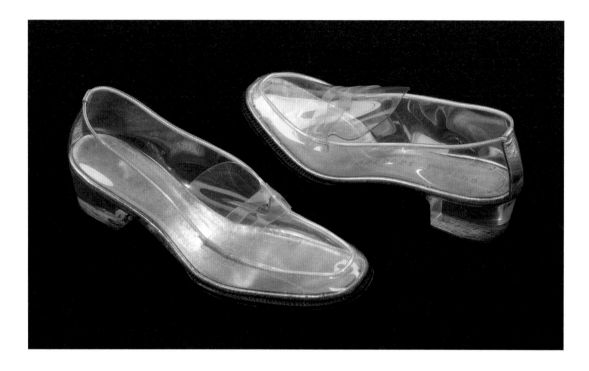

Mary Poppins

(English or American)

Shoes, ca. 1973

Pink, brown, and tan kidskin; label: "MG/ Mary Poppins/Made in Italy"
Brooklyn Museum Costume Collection at The Metropolitan Museum of Art, Gift of the Brooklyn Museum, 2009; Gift of Sheri Sandler, 1993 (2009.300.3392a, b)

The historicizing hippie look, which overtook fashion in the late 1960s, spurred the revival of the platform sole in 1967. Modern versions of the 1940s style had exaggerated bulgy toes, flaring heels, and curvaceous soles. Colorful piecing added a fresh graphic quality. In this example the two-tone scheme of the foresole and heel emphasizes the platform's height.

On the following pages is a selection from a group of more than seventy-five shoe prototypes, known in the industry as "pullovers," which are models formed over and nailed to wooden lasts, some completed with heels and some without. They were designed in Paris in 1939 by Steven Arpad. Arpad worked in Paris before World War II as the exclusive shoe designer for Balenciaga and for the U.S. firms Delman and I. Miller. He donated the prototypes along with an extensive archive of related drawings to the Brooklyn Museum in 1947. It is not known whether any of the designs were ever produced. However, the collection holds five pairs of finished Arpad shoes, two of which were documented through the sketch archive; they are included at the end of the section. Many of the lasts are annotated with design references. The materials document Arpad's creative process and his particular take on high-style couture shoe designs for 1939.

Steven Arpad
(French, born Hungary)

Shoe Prototype (Sandal), 1939

Dark brown suede; gold metallic kidskin; wood
Brooklyn Museum Costume Collection at
The Metropolitan Museum of Art, Gift of the
Brooklyn Museum, 2009; Gift of Arpad, 1947
(2009.300.1146)

Shoe Prototype, 1939

Dark brown suede; gold metallic kidskin; wood
Inscribed: "Thoughts on new basic form"
Brooklyn Museum Costume Collection at The Metropolitan Museum
of Art, Gift of the Brooklyn Museum, 2009; Gift of Arpad, 1947
(2009.300.1130)

Sketches, 1939
(pp. 245–249)

Crayon on paper, 24 x 26 cm. Brooklyn
Museum Costume Collection at The
Metropolitan Museum of Art, Gift of the
Brooklyn Museum, 2009; Gift of Arpad
1947. Courtesy of the Irene Lewsohn
Costume Reference Library

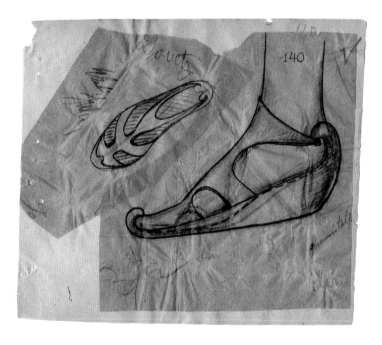

Shoe Prototype (Sandal), 1939

Periwinkle blue grained leather; wood
Brooklyn Museum Costume Collection at The Metropolitan Museum of Art,
Gift of the Brooklyn Museum, 2009; Gift of Arpad, 1947 (2009.300.1151)

Shoe Prototype, 1939

Violet suede piped in purple kidskin; wood
Inscribed: "Heel experiment/Weight -/+ slenderized ankle"
Brooklyn Museum Costume Collection at The Metropolitan Museum of Art,
Gift of the Brooklyn Museum, 2009; Gift of Arpad, 1947 (2009.300.1150)

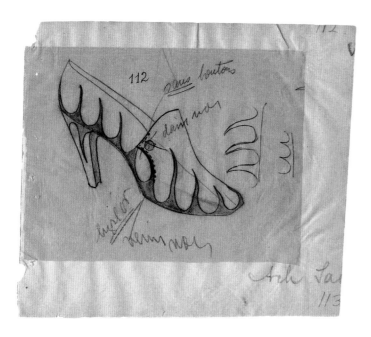

Steven Arpad

(French, born Hungary)

Shoe Prototype, 1939

Dark brown suede and patent leather piped in gold metallic kidskin; wood
Inscribed: "16 complication (of 6 & 13 or 14) new direction"
Brooklyn Museum Costume Collection at The Metropolitan Museum of Art,
Gift of the Brooklyn Museum, 2009; Gift of Arpad, 1947 (2009.300.1134)

Shoe Prototype, 1939

Dark brown suede; gold metallic kidskin; gold-tone metal oval buckle; wood
Inscribed: "Evolution from fusion of ideas-in color"
Brooklyn Museum Costume Collection at The Metropolitan Museum of Art,
Gift of the Brooklyn Museum, 2009; Gift of Arpad, 1947 (2009.300.1142)

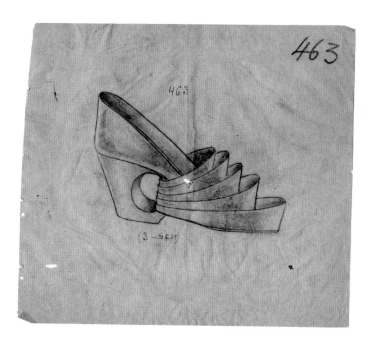

Shoe Prototype (Evening Pump), 1939

Black silk satin; gold metallic kidskin; wood
Inscribed: "Design flows (?) from front down to heel-this for theatre"
Brooklyn Museum Costume Collection at The Metropolitan Museum of Art,
Gift of the Brooklyn Museum, 2009; Gift of Arpad, 1947 (2009.300.1145)

Shoe Prototype, 1939

Light and dark teal lizard skin; bright blue kidskin; wood
Inscribed: "Heel different-decoration"
Brooklyn Museum Costume Collection at The Metropolitan Museum of Art,
Gift of the Brooklyn Museum, 2009; Gift of Arpad, 1947 (2009.300.1144)

Steven Arpad

(French, born Hungary)

Shoes, 1939

Black glazed kidskin; inscribed: "Colette"
Brooklyn Museum Costume Collection at The Metropolitan
Museum of Art, Gift of the Brooklyn Museum, 2009; Brooklyn
Museum Collection (2009.300.1393a, b)

Boots (Ankle Boots) 1939

Medium brown suede; dark brown glazed kidskin
Brooklyn Museum Costume Collection at The Metropolitan
Museum of Art, Gift of the Brooklyn Museum, 2009; Brooklyn
Museum Collection (2009.300.1392a, b)

For Cristobal Balenciaga (active 1935–1967)

Evening Shoes, 1938–1939

Black silk satin; black painted and carved wood arch forms
Brooklyn Museum Costume Collection at The Metropolitan
Museum of Art, Gift of the Brooklyn Museum, 2009; Brooklyn
Museum Collection (2009.300.1394a, b)

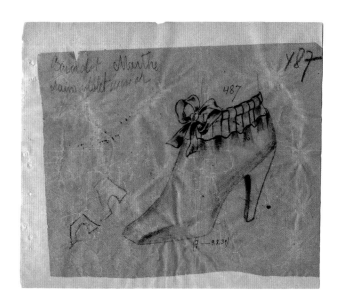

Evening Shoes, 1939

Black silk satin and patent leather; black painted and carved wood, Baroque scroll shapes
Brooklyn Museum Costume Collection at The Metropolitan Museum of Art, Gift of the Brooklyn Museum, 2009; Brooklyn Museum Collection (2009.300.1395a, b)

Evening Shoes, ca. 1940

Rust calfskin printed with green, light blue, and lavender orientalist patterning; peach and aqua metallic kidskin; label: "Delman/Paris-New York"
Brooklyn Museum Costume Collection at The Metropolitan Museum of Art, Gift of the Brooklyn Museum, 2009; Gift of Herman Delman, 1955 (2009.300.1205a, b)

Notes

Much of the information in this volume is the result of research and writing conducted by the Costume Documentation Project staff between 2005 and 2009. Introduction: Katie Netherton and Plácida Grace Hernández for Design Lab and Brooklyn Museum history. Historical Fashions: Elizabeth Randolph for changing silhouettes. French Couture: Jessa J. Krick for Virginia M. Prince and Rita de Acosta Lydig. Elsa Schiaparelli: Katie Netherton for Elsa Schiaparelli and Millicent Rogers. Women Designers: Jennifer K. Holley for Vera Maxwell, Katie Netherton for Jessie Franklin Turner, Plácida Grace Hernández and Deborah Saville for Sally Victor, Katherine M. Winters for Elizabeth Hawes, and Rachel Tu for Carolyn Schnurer. Charles James: Elizabeth Randolph for Austine Hearst. Rarities: Jessica G. Rall for Gratitude Train mannequins and Russian festive costumes. Shoes: Glenn Petersen for all shoes and the Charline Osgood collection. Substantial portions of the captions are paraphrases of his original writing.

Essays on these topics by the people mentioned above are held in the Brooklyn Museum Library collection.

Historical Costumes

1. James Laver, *The Concise History of Costume and Fashion* (New York: Harry N. Abrams, 1969), p. 179.
2. Regional costume was the early collecting focus. Fashion accessories were accepted, but not sought after, in the early part of the century starting in 1903.

The House of Worth

1. Brooklyn Museum Archives, Records Office of the Director (W. H. Fox, 1913–33), Gardiner, Edith (5/1926).
2. Ibid.
3. Much of the information for this chapter is based upon Elizabeth Ann Coleman's work on the subject, *The Opulent Era: Fashions of Worth, Doucet and Pingat* (New York: The Brooklyn Museum in association with Thames and Hudson, 1989), pp. 9–137.
4. "Breathe Oxygen and Be Thin," *New York Times*, February 2, 1909.
5. In a letter to Director W. H. Fox, dated February 4, 1921, held in the Brooklyn Museum Archives, Eleanor Hewitt writes of scrapbooks that she hopes he will find of interest.

French Couture

1. Pamela A. Parmal, "La Mode: Paris and the Development of the French Fashion Industry," in *Fashion Show: Paris Style* (Boston: MFA Publications, 2006), pp. 13–25.
2. Elizabeth Ann Coleman, *The Opulent Era: Fashions of Worth, Doucet and Pingat* (New York: The Brooklyn Museum in association with Thames and Hudson, 1989), pp. 143–45.
3. Ibid., p. 177.

Elsa Schiaparelli

1. Much of the information in this chapter is based upon Dilys Blum's authoritative work on the subject: *Shocking! The Art and Fashion of Elsa Schiaparelli* (Philadelphia: Philadelphia Museum of Art, 2003).

American Women Designers

1. An exception is Eta Hentz, who was less well known.
2. Jessie Franklin Turner was born in 1881. Eta Hentz's dates are not known. Pauline Trigère (1912–2002) was also of this generation and opened a business on New York's Seventh Avenue in 1942. Her influence on American fashion, however, was felt somewhat later than the women discussed here, and her best works are not represented in the Brooklyn collection.
3. Clare Potter (1892–1974) and Tina Lesser (1910–1986) also played a part in developing the American sportswear tradition.

American Men Designers

1. Source of both quotations: Brooklyn Museum Archives, Records of the Department of Costumes and Textiles, Objects Active, A; purchases accepted: Adrian, Janet Gaynor (1963).

Charles James

1. Brooklyn Museum Archives. Records of the Office of the Director (Edgar C. Schenck, 1955–59). Departments: Industrial Division (1956–57).
2. Bill Cunningham, "The Man," in *The Genius of Charles James* (New York: Holt, Rinehart, and Winston, 1982), p. 105.
3. In a letter to Director Charles Nagel dated March 5, 1952, James suggests that he arrange a luncheon with Mrs. Hearst. A follow-up letter dated March 21, confirms that it had taken place. Brooklyn Museum Archives. Records of the Office of the Director (Charles Nagel, 1946–1955). Departments: Industrial Design (1951–52).
4. The definitive work on the subject of Charles James is Elizabeth Ann Coleman, *The Genius of Charles James* (New York: Holt, Rinehart, and Winston, 1982). The author is a former curator of the Brooklyn Museum Costume Collection.

Rarities

1. Dilys E. Blum, *Ahead of Fashion: Hats of the 20th Century* (Philadelphia: Philadelphia Museum of Art, 1993), p. 27.
2. Michelle Murphy, *Two Centuries of French Fashion* (New York: Scribner, 1949).

Select Bibliography

Beaton, Cecil. *The Glass of Fashion*. Garden City, N.Y.: Doubleday, 1954.

Blum, Dilys E. *Ahead of Fashion: Hats of the 20th Century*. Philadelphia: Philadelphia Museum of Art, 1993.

Blum, Dilys E. *Shocking! The Art and Fashion of Elsa Schiaparelli*. Philadelphia: Philadelphia Museum of Art, 2003.

Bradley, Barry W. *Galanos*. Cleveland: Western Reserve Historical Society, 1996.

Charles-Roux, Edmonde, et al. *Théâtre de la Mode*. New York: Rizzoli, 1991.

Coleman, Elizabeth Ann. *The Genius of Charles James*. New York: Holt, Rinehart, and Winston, 1982.

Coleman, Elizabeth Ann. *The Opulent Era: Fashions of Worth, Doucet and Pingat*. Brooklyn: Brooklyn Museum in association with Thames and Hudson, 1989.

De La Haye, Amy, Lou Taylor, and Eleanor Thompson. *A Family of Fashion: The Messels: Six Generations of Dress*. London: Philip Wilson Publishers, 2005.

Esquevin, Christian. *Adrian: Silver Screen to Custom Label*. Foreword by Yeohlee. New York: Monacelli Press, 2008.

Fukai, Akiko, ed. *Fashion: The Collection of the Kyoto Costume Institute: A History from the 18th to the 20th Century*. Cologne: Taschen, 2002.

Holme, Charles, ed. *Peasant Art in Russia*. London: The Studio, 1912.

Jacobs, Laura. "Gowned for Glory." *Vanity Fair* (November 1998), pp. 114–29.

Kirke, Betty. *Madeleine Vionnet*. Foreword by Issye Miyake. San Francisco: Chronicle Books, 1998.

Laver, James. *The Concise History of Costume and Fashion*. New York: Harry N. Abrams, 1969.

Lee, Sarah Tomerlin, ed. *American Fashion: The Life and Lines of Adrian, Mainbocher, McCardell, Norell, and Trigère*. New York: Quadrangle, 1975.

Martin, Richard. *American Ingenuity: Sportswear, 1930s–1970s*. New York: Metropolitan Museum of Art, 1998.

Martin, Richard. *Charles James*. London: Thames and Hudson, 1997.

Martin, Richard. *Fashion and Surrealism*. New York: Rizzoli, 1987.

Martin, Richard, and Harold Koda. *Christian Dior*. New York: Metropolitan Museum of Art, 1996.

Martin, Richard, and Harold Koda. *Haute Couture*. New York: Metropolitan Museum of Art, 1995.

Mears, Patricia. *Madame Grès: The Sphinx of Fashion*. New Haven: Yale University Press, 2007.

Merceron, Dean L. *Lanvin*. Foreword by Alber Elbaz. Introduction by Harold Koda. New York: Rizzoli, 2007.

Milbank, Caroline Rennolds. *Couture: The Great Designers*. New York: Stewart, Tabori & Chang, 1985.

Milbank, Caroline Rennolds. *New York Fashion: The Evolution of American Style*. New York: Harry N. Abrams, 1989.

Miller, Lesley Ellis. *Cristóbal Balenciaga (1895–1972): The Couturiers' Couturier*. London: V&A Publications, 2007.

O'Keeffe, Linda. *Shoes: A Celebration of Pumps, Sandals, Slippers & More*. New York: Workman Publishing, 1996.

Olian, JoAnne. *The House of Worth: The Gilded Age, 1860–1918*. New York: Museum of the City of New York, 1982.

Palmer, Alexandra. *Couture & Commerce: The Transatlantic Fashion Trade in the 1950s*. Vancouver: UBC Press, 2001.

Parmal, Pamela A., and Didier Grumbach. *Fashion Show: Paris Style*. Boston: MFA Publications, 2006.

Riello, Giorgio, and Peter McNeil, eds. *Shoes: A History from Sandals to Sneakers*. Oxford: Berg, 2006.

Shaeffer, Claire B. *Couture Sewing: Techniques*. Newtown, Conn.: Taunton Press, 1993.

Steele, Valerie. *Paris Fashion: A Cultural History*. New York: Oxford University Press, 1988.

Steele, Valerie. *Women of Fashion: Twentieth-Century Designers*. New York: Rizzoli International, 1991.

Thieme, Otto Charles, et al. *With Grace & Favour: Victorian & Edwardian Fashion in America*. Cincinnati: Cincinnati Art Museum, 1993.

Walford, Jonathan. *The Seductive Shoe: Four Centuries of Fashion Footwear*. New York: Stewart, Tabori & Chang, 2007.

White, Palmer. *Elsa Schiaparelli: Empress of Paris Fashion*. Foreword by Yves Saint Laurent. New York: Rizzoli, 1986.

Yohannan, Kohle. *Valentina: American Couture and the Cult of Celebrity*. Foreword by Harold Koda. New York: Rizzoli, 2009.

Yohannan, Kohle, and Nancy Nolf. *Claire McCardell: Redefining Modernism*. New York: Harry N. Abrams, 1998.

Alternate Accession Numbers

MMA	BM	MMA	BM	MMA	BM	MMA	BM
2009.300.6a–e	41.199a-c	2009.300.512	74.185.10	2009.300.941a–e	70.53.5a-e	2009.300.1164	51.33.23
2009.300.29a–c	67.171.2a-b	2009.300.517	75.102.3	2009.300.948a–c	71.164.2a-c	2009.300.1165a, b	51.33.35a-b
2009.300.44	CP822	2009.300.527	78.75.19	2009.300.980a, b	77.37.37a-b	2009.300.1168a–c	51.33.46a-c
2009.300.64	26.375	2009.300.531a–c	79.166.4a-c	2009.300.991	81.25.3	2009.300.1169a, b	51.33.43, .50
2009.300.94	41.910	2009.300.545	83.87.9	2009.300.997	83.19.4	2009.300.1174	52.96.4
2009.300.118a, b	46.20.2a-b	2009.300.576	1989.98.1	2009.300.999	83.23.2	2009.300.1175	53.68.8
2009.300.119	46.20.5	2009.300.585a–d	1993.202.5a-d	2009.300.1000a, b	83.46a-b	2009.300.1178a, b	53.267.14.1a-b
2009.300.140	50.72.14	2009.300.586	1993.202.6	2009.300.1009	84.60.5	2009.300.1181	53.267.27
2009.300.141	50.72.32	2009.300.589	1993.202.9	2009.300.1041a–c	88.97.5a-e	2009.300.1184a, b	54.63.36a-b
2009.300.145	51.27.81	2009.300.600	1996.173.7	2009.300.1063a, b	1991.88.1a-b	2009.300.1187	54.141.73
2009.300.146	51.33.28	2009.300.622a–c	26.372a-c	2009.300.1093a–e	26.356a-c	2009.300.1193	54.169.13
2009.300.161a, b	52.62.A.30a-b	2009.300.640a–g	31.103.1.5-.7, .9, .10, .13a-b	2009.300.1100a, b	31.27a-b	2009.300.1196a–d	54.205a-e
2009.300.180	54.141.74	2009.300.643a, b	32.1708a-b	2009.300.1101	31.452	2009.300.1200	54.207.9
2009.300.190	54.141.99	2009.300.664a, b	41.913a-b	2009.300.1103	31.465	2009.300.1202	54.207.12
2009.300.195a, b	54.170.2a-b	2009.300.668	42.207.16	2009.300.1104	31.467	2009.300.1205a, b	55.16.32a-b
2009.300.229a, b	56.166.2a-b	2009.300.674	44.179	2009.300.1105	31.469	2009.300.1206a, b	55.16.33a-b
2009.300.231a–c	56.166.13a-c	2009.300.687	48.199.1	2009.300.1106	31.470	2009.300.1207a, b	55.16.47a-b
2009.300.265	59.146.26	2009.300.700a–c	49.139.11	2009.300.1110a, b	33.74a-b	2009.300.1210	55.26.22
2009.300.268	59.158	2009.300.701a–c	49.139.12	2009.300.1111	38.93	2009.300.1212	55.26.25
2009.300.270a–d	59.163a-d	2009.300.711	49.139.22	2009.300.1112	41.786	2009.300.1224	55.26.142
2009.300.274	60.86.1	2009.300.714a–d	49.139.25	2009.300.1117	44.105.25	2009.300.1225	55.26.144
2009.300.299	61.137	2009.300.719a, b	49.139.30	2009.300.1119	44.105.32	2009.300.1226	55.26.151
2009.300.305	61.176.5	2009.300.720a–e	49.139.31	2009.300.1127	47.102.5	2009.300.1227	55.26.153
2009.300.319	63.18.1	2009.300.722	49.139.33	2009.300.1130	47.102.10	2009.300.1234	55.26.247
2009.300.320	63.18.2	2009.300.726a, b	49.139.37a-b	2009.300.1134	47.102.16	2009.300.1236	55.26.258
2009.300.344a–e	64.134.4a-e	2009.300.727a–c	49.139.39	2009.300.1139	47.102.30	2009.300.1237	55.26.259
2009.300.345	64.134.6	2009.300.734	49.233.18	2009.300.1142	47.102.41	2009.300.1242	55.194.14
2009.300.377	65.189.4	2009.300.779	53.169.1	2009.300.1144	47.102.46	2009.300.1244a, b	56.64.4a-b
2009.300.382	65.222.22a-b	2009.300.788a, b	54.141.24a-b	2009.300.1145	47.102.49	2009.300.1245a–c	56.166.4a-c
2009.300.391a, b	65.268.31a-b	2009.300.795	54.141.90	2009.300.1146	47.102.51	2009.300.1251a, b	57.104a-b
2009.300.450a, b	67.215.4a-b	2009.300.810a, b	57.30a-b	2009.300.1150	47.102.59	2009.300.1256a, b	58.55.11a-b
2009.300.454	67.245.36	2009.300.816	57.109.1	2009.300.1151	47.102.63	2009.300.1261a, b	60.195.6a-b
2009.300.459a–g	68.78.1a-f	2009.300.832	59.39	2009.300.1153a, b	49.46.17a-b	2009.300.1269a, b	60.195.87a-b
2009.300.462	68.196.1	2009.300.849	61.42.16	2009.300.1155a–l	49.144.1a-j	2009.300.1270a, b	60.195.95a-b
2009.300.466a–c	69.33.10a-c	2009.300.872	64.41.2	2009.300.1157a, b	50.40.4a-b	2009.300.1278a–c	60.219.1a-c
2009.300.510a–c	74.185.7a-c	2009.300.903a, b	66.169.1a-b	2009.300.1161	50.175.5	2009.300.1289	61.176.2
2009.300.511a–c	74.185.8a-c	2009.300.922	69.2.17	2009.300.1162	51.27.116	2009.300.1294	62.94.5

MMA	BM	MMA	BM	MMA	BM	MMA	BM
2009.300.1295a, b	62.167.29a-b	2009.300.1410a, b	28.102.15a-b	2009.300.1710	31.306	2009.300.2117a, b	67.110.142a-b
2009.300.1297a, b	63.18.4a-b	2009.300.1419	31.463	2009.300.1712	31.378	2009.300.2144a–d	69.33.32.1a-b
2009.300.1299	63.23.5	2009.300.1436a–g	45.57.1-.6a-b	2009.300.1718	31.477	2009.300.2149a–c	69.101.1.1
2009.300.1300a–f	63.23.6a-f	2009.300.1439a–d	46.36.9a-b	2009.300.1719	31.478	2009.300.2176a–c	73.20.2a-c
2009.300.1311	64.109.1	2009.300.1445a–d	49.139.38	2009.300.1803a, b	46.151.1	2009.300.2186	77.252
2009.300.1318a, b	64.126.7a-b	2009.300.1446	51.33.8	2009.300.1806	47.223.2	2009.300.2191a, b	80.35.4a-b
2009.300.1320	64.255.8	2009.300.1148	47.102.56	2009.300.1830	49.221.1	2009.300.2198a, b	83.23.1
2009.300.1321	64.255.10	2009.300.1459a, b	53.267.17a-b	2009.300.1846a, b	52.62.A.10a-b	2009.300.2212	85.142
2009.300.1324a, b	65.189.2a-b	2009.300.1463a, b	54.61.31a-b	2009.300.1852	53.267.1	2009.300.2228a, b	88.102a-b
2009.300.1331a–e	67.110.95a-e	2009.300.1473a, b	54.61.46a-b	2009.300.1857	54.141.38	2009.300.2230a, b	1989.151.3a-b
2009.300.1333a, b	67.110.117a-b	2009.300.1484a, b	54.61.114a-b	2009.300.1858	54.141.40	2009.300.2239a, b	1994.40.1a-b
2009.300.1334	67.110.120	2009.300.1486a, b	54.61.149a-b	2009.300.1860	54.141.86	2009.300.2240a, b	1994.40.8a-b
2009.300.1347a, b	69.33.8a-b	2009.300.1488a–f	54.61.152a-d	2009.300.1861	54.141.93	2009.300.2242a–c	1996.173.8a-c
2009.300.1350a–c	69.149.11a-c	2009.300.1494a, b	55.16.52a-b	2009.300.1866	54.141.213	2009.300.2244	CP18
2009.300.1354	71.67	2009.300.1505a, b	56.64.3a-b	2009.300.1867	54.141.214	2009.300.2245	CP34
2009.300.1363a, b	83.98.3a-b	2009.300.1507	56.170.5	2009.300.1868	54.141.215	2009.300.2261	X178
2009.300.1365	84.30	2009.300.1555a, b	65.188.4a-b	2009.300.1869	55.26.26	2009.300.2267	69.33.13
2009.300.1372a–d	87.115a-d	2009.300.1580a, b	67.110.73a-b	2009.300.1870a, b	55.26.38a-b	2009.300.2323a–d	31.449
2009.300.1373	88.97.6	2009.300.1581a, b	67.110.77a-b	2009.300.1892a, b	55.144.15a-b	2009.300.2497	61.186.2
2009.300.1383a, b	1990.23.3a-b	2009.300.1584a, b	67.110.259c-d	2009.300.1900a–c	56.129.100a-c	2009.300.2611	75.101.1
2009.300.1388a, b	1995.10a-b	2009.300.1612a, b	81.107.1a-b	2009.300.1935	57.112.5	2009.300.2786	54.141.91
2009.300.1389a–e	1995.53a-e	2009.300.1614a, b	83.87.7a-b	2009.300.2010	61.241.11	2009.300.2787	54.141.94
2009.300.1392a, b	CP435a-b	2009.300.1633a, b	1993.63.2a-b	2009.300.2031a–c	63.120.10a-c	2009.300.2923	86.120.3
2009.300.1393a, b	CP436a-b	2009.300.1664	22.47	2009.300.2033a–e	63.212a-e	2009.300.3136a, b	51.33.73a-b
2009.300.1394a, b	X1025.1a-b	2009.300.1677	24.416.4	2009.300.2043a–c	65.34.20a-c	2009.300.3265a, b	64.236.2a-b
2009.300.1395a, b	X1025.2a-b	2009.300.1681	26.383	2009.300.2055	66.9.22	2009.300.3375a, b	85.205.14a-b
2009.300.1404a, b	24.443a-b	2009.300.1690a, b	29.1131.4	2009.300.2115a, b	67.110.98a-b	2009.300.3381a, b	86.8.1a-b
2009.300.1407a, b	28.102.7a-b	2009.300.1708	31.22	2009.300.2116	67.110.131	2009.300.3392a, b	1993.26.1a-b

Acknowledgments

A host of people associated with the Brooklyn Museum and The Metropolitan Museum of Art lent their expertise, support, and guidance in making the Costume Documentation Project, this publication, and the two exhibitions that accompany it a reality. I acknowledge and offer sincere thanks to all those who could not be mentioned here by name.

Particular appreciation and gratitude are extended to Arnold Lehman, Director of the Brooklyn Museum; Kevin Stayton, Chief Curator; Ken Moser, Vice Director for Collections; Carol Lee Shen, Chief Conservator; Judith Frankfurt, Deputy Director for Administration; Charles Desmarais, Deputy Director for Art; David Kleiser, former Vice Director for Finance and Administration; Cynthia Mayeda, Deputy Director for Institutional Advancement; Rob Krulak, Senior Project Manager, Curatorial Initiatives; and Angelica Rudenstine, Andrew W. Mellon Foundation Program Officer, whose enormous contributions at the inception of the project and their continued guidance have made possible all that has transpired in the last six years.

For their expertise and support in establishing the landmark partnership with the Brooklyn Museum, gratitude is also extended to Philippe de Montebello, former Director of The Metropolitan Museum of Art; Thomas P. Campbell, Director; Emily K. Rafferty, President; Nina McN. Diefenbach, Vice President for Development and Membership; Chris Coulson, Senior Advisor to the Director; Doralynn Pines, former Associate Director for Administration; Harold Koda, Curator in Charge of the Costume Institute; Andrew Bolton, Curator, Costume Institute; and Chris Paulocik, Conservator, Costume Institute.

The thirteen members of the Brooklyn Museum Costume Documentation Project staff, whose professional work is embodied in every page of this book, deserve special recognition and my deepest gratitude: most particularly Elizabeth Fiorentino, Collections Manager, who, with great intelligence, skill, and patience performed, among other tasks, the miracle of keeping track of the 24,000 objects as they moved through the four-stage process of evaluation; Glenn Petersen, Conservator, who heroically and skillfully dressed and styled over 3,000 objects, catalogued the shoes, and, along with the collections manager, oversaw the well-being of the collection; and Plácida Grace Hernández, Assistant Curator, who contributed her considerable research, editing, and writing skills to the style, format, and content of the database records and to the preparation of the essays prepared at the end of project; and also Senior Research Assistant Jessa J. Krick and Research Assistants Jennifer K. Holley, Katie Netherton, Elizabeth Randolph, Jessica G. Rall, Deborah Saville, Rachel Tu, and Katherine M. Winters, all of whom set the highest standards of excellence in performing multiple tasks, which included data entry, photography, object preparation, research, and writing; and finally to photographers Lea Ingold and Lolly Koon, whose exquisite work is presented here. Gratitude is also extended to photographer Ellen Warfield, who seamlessly substituted during Lolly Koon's short absence; to Milton Sonday, who lent his incomparable expertise to cataloging the laces; and to former curators Elizabeth Ann Coleman and Patricia Mears, whose scholarship was the foundation for our work.

For the myriad ways in which they assisted and supported the Costume Project and this book, sincere appreciation goes to the following Brooklyn Museum staff members: Walter Andersons, Collections Manager; Jim Kelly, Manager of Security; Frantz Vincent, Vice Director of Operations; Deborah Wythe, Head of Digital Collections and Services; Digital Imaging Specialists Sarah Gentile, Alana Corbett, Katherine Hausenbauer, and Anita Cruz-Eberhard, who expertly managed the nearly 30,000 images produced during the project; staff photographer Sarah Kraemer; Shelley Bernstein, Technology Chief; and computer support specialists Dale Ramsey and Bob Nardi; Liz Reynolds, Chief Registrar; Terri O'Hara, Associate Registrar; Toni Owen, Senior Paper Conservator; Deirdre Lawrence, Principal Librarian; Angie Park, Archivist; Sandy Wallace, Librarian; Chrisy Ledakis, Records Manager; Stephanie Leverock, former Records Manager; Allison Galland, Collections Review Assistant; Robert Barclay, Supervising Museum Guard; Al Conca, Assistant Museum Maintainer; and Rosa Vega, Custodial Assistant.

Particular recognition is offered to the following Brooklyn Museum staff for their contributions to the exhibition "American High Style: Fashioning a National Identity": Matthew Yokobosky, Chief Designer; Jennifer Bantz, Interpretive Materials Manager; John

Antonides, Editor; Megan Doyle Carmody, Exhibitions Manager; Cheri Ehrlich, Ed.M., Senior Museum Educator/Teen Programs Coordinator; Radiah Harper, Vice-Director for Education and Program Development; and Traslin Ong, Manager of Adult Programs.

For their invaluable contributions to this publication and the accompanying exhibitions, my thanks are extended to the following staff members at The Metropolitan Museum of Art: Sharon Cott, Vice President, Secretary, and General Counsel; Rebecca Gideon, James Moske, and Romy Vreeland, Counsel's Office; Aileen K. Chuk, Registrar; and Willa Cox, Emily Foss, Nesta Mayo, Megan Porzio, Registrar's Office.

My special gratitude and appreciation go to the members of the Editorial Department, whose individual and collective interest, support, inspired ideas, and attention to detail have greatly enriched and given form to this publication: John P. O'Neill, former Publisher and Editor in Chief; Gwen Roginsky, General Manager of Publications; Bruce Campbell, Designer; Margaret Chace, Managing Editor; Mary Jo Mace, Administrator; Douglas Malicki, Production Manager; and Carol Liebowitz and Robert Weisberg, Desktop Publishing. Special acknowledgment and gratitude go to editor Joan Holt, for her inspiration, patience, and expert guidance.

Wholehearted thanks and appreciation are also extended to the members of the Costume Institute staff for their enthusiastic support and professional assistance: most especially to Joyce Fung and Shannon Price, Curatorial; Elizabeth Bryan, Senior Research Associate and Collections Manager, who with her team accomplished the daunting task of physically relocating the collection; and Nancy Chilton, Senior Press Officer for the Costume Institute. Also to Elizabeth Abbarno, Carolina Bermudez, Michael Downer, Patty Edmonson, Kathy Francis, Cassandra Gero, Jessica Glasscock, Amanda Haskins, Stéphane Houy-Towner, Mark Joseph, Heather Knapp, Julie Lê, Meghan Lee, Bethany Matia, Brigid Merriman, Marci Morimoto, Won Ng, Jennifer Park, Jessica Regan, Emily Ripley, Lita Semerad, Suzanne Shapiro, Kristen Stewart, Yer Vang, and Kirsta Willis; and to Kohle Yohannan for his early support and guidance.

For their specialized expertise, my sincere thanks go to Martin Bansbach and Rachel Mustalish in Paper Conservation; Jennie Choi, Collections Management/TMS; Andrew Gessner, Shyam Oberoi, Danny Rotondo, Koven Smith, and Adam Padron, Information Systems and Technology; Aimee Dixon and Joseph Loh, Education Department; Mia Fineman and Lucy von Brachel, Department of Photographs; Will Lach and Elizabeth Stoneman, Merchandising Department; the Thomas J. Watson Library; the Image Library; and the Photograph Studio.

Costume Institute interns are also to be thanked: Katie Deane, Michel Fox, Eustacia Huen, Allison Johnson, Lisa Kobs, Marcella Milio, Silvia de Miranda, Jennifer Moore, Brian Nussbaum, Rebecca Perry, Anne Reilly, Emily Toxie, Lalena Vellano; docents and volunteers Marie Arnold, Kitty Benton, Barbara Brickman, Jane Butler, Patricia Corbin, Eileen Ekstract, Ruth Henderson, Elizabeth Kehler, Susan Klein, Rena Lustberg, Butzi Moffitt, Ellen Needham, Wendy Nolan, Patricia Peterson, Phyllis Potter, Rena Schklowsky, Eleanore Schloss, Bernice Shaftan, Nancy Silbert, Judith Sommer, Andrea Vizcarrondo, DJ White; and wig preparators Meredith Burns, Elizabeth DeSole, and Donna Tsui.

I am extremely grateful to the Friends of The Costume Institute, Lizzie Tisch, Chair, and The Visiting Committee of The Costume Institute for their ongoing support.

The following photo agencies and individuals are also recognized for their contributions and prompt responses to requests for images: Barry Friedman Gallery (Karen Gilbert); Sotheby's Picture Library; Brooklyn Museum (Ruth Janson, Beth Kushner); The Everett Collection; Condé Nast Publications (Katherine Aguilera, Alex Ebrahimi-Navissi, Gretchen Fenston, Dawn Lucas, Leigh Montville, Shawn Waldron); Center for Creative Photography (Tammy Carter); Hugo Vickers; Jerry Murbach (www.doctormacro.info); Photofest; Getty Images; Corbis; Art Resource; Elizabeth Randolph; Glenn Petersen; Hearst Magazines (Wendy Israel); The Picture Desk; and Artists Rights Society.

For their long-term support I extend my deep gratitude to Mike Glier, Martin Kamer, and Nina Wegener.